The Long-Distance Teammate

The Long-Distance Teammate

Stay Engaged and Connected
While Working Anywhere

Kevin Eikenberry and Wayne Turmel

Berrett–Koehler Publishers, Inc.

Berrett-Koehler Publishers, Inc.
1333 Broadway, Suite 1000
Oakland, CA 94612-1921
Tel: (510) 817-2277
Fax: (510) 817-2278
www.bkconnection.com

ORDERING INFORMATION
Quantity sales. Special discounts are available on quantity purchases by corporations, associations, and others. For details, contact the "Special Sales Department" at the Berrett-Koehler address above.
Individual sales. Berrett-Koehler publications are available through most bookstores. They can also be ordered directly from Berrett-Koehler: Tel: (800) 929-2929; Fax: (802) 864-7626; www.bkconnection.com.
Orders for college textbook / course adoption use. Please contact Berrett-Koehler:
Tel: (800) 929-2929; Fax: (802) 864-7626.

Distributed to the U.S. trade and internationally by Penguin Random House Publisher Services.

Berrett-Koehler and the BK logo are registered trademarks of Berrett-Koehler Publishers, Inc.

Printed in the United States of America.

Berrett-Koehler books are printed on long-lasting acid-free paper. When it is available, we choose paper that has been manufactured by environmentally responsible processes. These may include using trees grown in sustainable forests, incorporating recycled paper, minimizing chlorine in bleaching, or recycling the energy produced at the paper mill.

Library of Congress Cataloging-in-Publication Data
Names: Eikenberry, Kevin, 1962- author. | Turmel, Wayne, author.
Title: The long-distance teammate : stay engaged and connected while
  working anywhere / Kevin Eikenberry and Wayne Turmel.
Description: First edition. | Oakland, CA : Berrett-Koehler Publishers,
  Inc., [2020] | Includes bibliographical references and index.
Identifiers: LCCN 2020037957 | ISBN 9781523090303 (paperback ; alk. paper)
  | ISBN 9781523090310 (adobe pdf) | ISBN 9781523090327 (epub)
Subjects: LCSH: Virtual work teams. | Telecommuting. | Career development.
Classification: LCC HD66 .E35 2020 | DDC 650.1--dc23
LC record available at https://lccn.loc.gov/2020037957

First Edition
26 25 24 23 22 21 20   10 9 8 7 6 5 4 3 2 1

Book producer and text designer: Happenstance Type-O-Rama
Cover designer: Adrian Morgan

To Parker, Kelsey, and Nora
You'll work in ways your dads never dreamed of

Contents

Contents

Introduction

The trend toward remote work is undeniable and is happening in more and more types of jobs. Whether you are new to remote work, or are an old hand, odds are you've picked up this book for one of these reasons:

- You plan to start or are thinking about working remotely and want to succeed.

- You work remotely and want to be as successful as you can be (and perhaps know you have room for improvement).

- Your organization is moving your role to work from home or away from the office.

- You are a contract or gig worker but want to be more valuable—and get more contracts and gigs.

- You lead (or will be leading) remote team members and as a part of the team want to help them succeed (you are a part of that team—and probably another remote team too).

Whichever of these groups you find yourself in, you're in the right place. In writing this book, we have been thinking about each of you and plan to give you practical, principle-based solutions to the challenges you face, or will face, as a part of a long-distance, virtual, or remote team.

The World Has Changed

This book was conceived and mostly written before anyone had heard of coronavirus or could fathom what would happen to the workplace and the way we work in the blink of an eye. The trend toward more remote work had been building for years, but in a moment, nearly anyone who might be able to work from home was doing it. The experiences the world has faced prove many of our points and make them more real and important.

A key idea for this book is now real for most of us—*there is a big difference between working from home and feeling like and being an effective member of a remote team*. This isn't a book about working from home. It is a book about being a great teammate while working at a distance from those you must collaborate with.

Even after the initial COVID-19 response, you're likely facing new ways of working. Even if you return to the office, it may be only part time, or the person at the next desk who has been there for ages may not be there some or most of the time. Being a teammate will look very different than it did not too long ago and will continue to evolve. If everyone on the team isn't face-to-face every day, this book is for all of you.

About Us—Your Guides on This Journey

We come to the table with real-life experience. Wayne has worked as part of a remote team, and often from home, for most of his business career. Originally, he was in an office far from his teammates. Now he works for The Kevin Eikenberry Group primarily from a home office, thousands of miles, and a couple of time zones, from his geographically nearest teammate. Kevin has been helping leaders grow and change and adapt to the needs of their organizations and teams for nearly thirty years—most of those as the leader of The Kevin Eikenberry Group. He too is a member of a remote team and leads this team every day. Together we formed the Remote Leadership Institute and wrote the book you might consider the precursor to this one—*The Long-Distance Leader: Rules for Remarkable Remote Leadership*.

We live what we write about. We approach this book as thought leaders, because we have thought deeply about the challenges and opportunities in this book. Also consider us results leaders—pointing you to practical ways to be more successful and get better results every day. While we and our team are far from perfect, we've learned what works and we are doing everything we can to achieve what we believe you can achieve too.

Who This Book Is For

The ideas that follow will do more than relieve the stress and frustrations that come from remote working arrangements and help you and your team succeed at levels you haven't perhaps considered or thought possible.

Working remotely isn't just a new normal—something we must learn to live with—it is an opportunity to work in ways that provide great operational and productivity results for the organization, as well as provide individual teammates with the opportunity to be a part of great results while finding great meaning for themselves too.

Being a Long-Distance Teammate covers a variety of situations. It could mean being part of a team that will never meet face-to-face, or of a team that sees each other a few times a year. It includes what we call the hybrid team, where some work in the same location, and others work elsewhere. The mindsets, skillsets, and habitsets you need to succeed as a part of a team in any of these situations are more similar than different, and this book is for you in any of these circumstances.

It also doesn't matter where you work in the world or if you are part time, a gig worker, or on a long-term contract. The ideas we share here will help you regardless of your work classification and location. What we will address and help you with applies across times zones, cultures, and working situations.

This book will give you a new perspective on what remote work can be, set a higher benchmark, and help you create a work life that supports the rest of your life too.

A Note about Terminology

Some people distinguish between a manager and a leader, based on style or approach. We believe regardless of your organization level, if you have others who report to you, you have both leadership responsibilities and management responsibilities. Regardless of how you feel about these two words as descriptors of a role, they are often considered synonyms.

Because we believe the leadership parts of the role are more complex and too often lacking, we (especially Kevin) prefer to use the word *leader*. In this book, however, for readability purposes we are using the words *leader, manager*, and *boss* interchangeably.

Three Key Words

The title and subtitle of this book were chosen intentionally; there are three words, *teammate, connected*, and *engaged*, we needed to include because they are critical to successful, satisfying remote work.

- *Teammate.* Consulting several dictionaries led to the same definition of this word—*a member of a team.* Yet with all respect to those who write dictionaries, we believe there is a difference between a team member and a teammate.

  To our thinking, seeing yourself as a team member can be deceptively simple—anyone who shares a manager or works on the same project is a team member. Too often this is where people working remotely end up. Just because you've been assigned to a team doesn't mean you know the other members well or understand the interconnections between your work. While you report to a manager with other team members, in practice you may feel like a lone wolf, laser-focused and working on what you've been assigned. While this mindset is understandable, it serves you, the team, and the organization poorly.

  We see a true teammate as something different and deeper than that. To be a teammate implies a social and emotional connection that goes beyond merely who you report to and work with. Being a teammate implies a deeper level of commitment to, and connection with, others and the outcomes of the team. In some parts of the world the word *mate* has the connotation of friend or someone close to you. While we aren't saying you must be friends with those you work with, it does happen (though less often when working remotely). The implication is clear—when you view your role and relationships with others as more than just transactional, better, more satisfying results can occur. While this difference between *team member* and *teammate* can exist in traditional working environments, it is even more likely when people are apart from each other. This difference drives a big part of the point and value of the book and shows why we take the word so seriously.

- *Connected.* You might be thinking about *connected* from a technology perspective. After all, it is technology that has fueled the shift to people working from home, coffee shops, airports, and wherever they might be. And while technology is part of this puzzle, being connected means far more than having a strong Wi-Fi signal and the right apps loaded on your devices.

  Being connected as a Long-Distance Teammate means connection to the work, your boss, the direction of the organization, and your fellow teammates, more than just technical connections, but interpersonal ones.

- *Engaged.* Few words are bigger buzzwords in business and organizational literature than *engagement*. Books are written for and conference keynotes are delivered to leaders to help them engage their teams as if it is something you do to them. While we agree there are many things a leader can do to encourage, support, and promote engaged teams, we think that misses much of the point. It certainly misses the point of this book. Engagement isn't something that is done to you—it is something you choose to do.

  Engagement is more than employee satisfaction. You can be satisfied, and your job's fine. Nothing's wrong, but it doesn't mean that you're engaged. Engaged is a level of caring beyond just "It's okay." How much discretionary effort are you putting in? How much of your heart, soul, and effort are you putting into your work? Are you satisfied with just the bare minimum, or are you doing your best most of the time?

  Contrary to popular opinion, we believe your engagement largely belongs to you. How much you care, how hard you try, how much effort you put into your work, is in your control—all of these are your choices. Can those around you (including your boss) make those choices easier or harder? Sure—but the choices are still yours. There will be good and bad days. The network is going to go down. People are sometimes annoying.

Your boss is going to sometimes ask things of you that you just can't do. None of that is inside your control. But you can control how you react to it and how engaged you remain.

We want you to choose to be engaged in your work as a remote teammate. We believe that everyone (you, the rest of your team, your leadership, and the organization as a whole) wins when this happens. We want to help you see the choice and make that choice practically and tactically every day. While we spend much of our time helping leaders do their part, no one wins while you wait for them. You win when you choose to be engaged.

Why Engagement?

This point is too important, and too different from what you have considered before, to dive into without a bit more conversation. When you choose to be engaged, you:

- *Enjoy your work more.* You're not just going through the motions. You're not just doing the bare minimum. When you are enjoying yourself, when you're challenged, when you care, you're likely to do more and better work.

- *See a bigger picture.* When you are too focused on your work, you can lose perspective—and see the tree but not the forest. When you intentionally expand your view, you begin to see how your work relates to others and you care about the greater success—for yourself, your teammates, and the organization. You're thinking about the big picture as well as your daily task details. With this bigger view and a better understanding of how you fit in, you will become even more engaged.

- *Build stronger relationships.* Whether you really value having close working relationships, or just would like less drama in your workday, you will agree that relationships matter. Some of us create connections with our peers and colleagues naturally—for others it's hard work—but there's no doubt that they are harder to build remotely. We'll give you plenty to help you, but for now just remember that when you are engaged this will come more easily, in part because you realize your role in making it happen.

- *See and seize opportunities.* Remember that leaders are looking for and value those who are engaged. Choosing to engage is the first step in being viewed differently, as someone who deserves and will succeed at a special project or assignment, or even a promotion. You won't miss out on opportunities for advancement, recognition, or growing your skills. You're going to grab those chances to show what you can do. And as you can see, if you are fully engaged, you're going to be a much better teammate.

- *Get noticed.* One of the biggest challenges and complaints about working remotely is that you can become invisible. There's plenty in what follows about how to do this well, but for now realize that when you choose to engage with others and be engaged, this will be easier and, in many cases, will come far more naturally.

It will take focus and work to achieve the picture we have just described. The rest of this book points the way and will encourage you. Let's go.

Part 1

You as a Remote Teammate

Allison is a contractor working on a project team based in Chicago, even though she lives in Denver. This isn't her first remote assignment, so she knows some days are better than others. Sometimes she's motivated and active; sometimes it's all she can do to get through her to-do list. There are a few people on the team she's gotten to know well enough to joke with, and those are the people she goes to when she needs information or just human contact. Most days she's positive and ready to go; other days it can be isolating and a little lonely.

By definition, a team is "a group of people with a full set of complementary skills required to complete a task, job, or project."[1]

Whether you are a full-time remote worker or just do it a couple of days a week to get things done and off your list, you know the importance of being part of a team. When you work in the same location as everyone else—or even just some of your group—it's easy to feel like you're not alone in the world. People chit-chat in the break room, or you see people three cubicles over (and sometimes hear them, which is one of the reasons you like working alone!) and can ask questions or get information in a hurry.

There is a palpable energy to the traditional workplace that isn't there when you work at a distance. On one hand, that energy can sometimes be overwhelming—too much noise, chatter, gossip, and too many distractions.

That's why many of us enjoy working somewhere quiet. On the other hand, when you toil alone you are your own energy source.

Yes, it's quiet and you can get work done, and that's great, at least for a while.

The tricky thing is that when you are by yourself, you are your own energy source, and your mental batteries are called on to generate a lot of energy. If you're not careful, those resources can be quickly drained.

Maybe you're already feeling this. Some days you feel isolated and alone. You seem to be working harder than ever and not getting the right things checked off your task list. Other days you bang the work out and still have time to walk the dog before it's too dark. Some days you're getting all the information you need and you're able to respond immediately to requests for help. Other times your cries for help go into a black hole, or it takes you forever (and you might even forget completely) to respond to a request for information.

Some of us require a fair amount of human contact or we go crazy. Even introverts who prefer to be left alone much of the time (in fact, that's how they recharge their batteries) can't get everything done without other people and can't be truly great teammates without being available and helpful to others.

That's the paradox of remote work. You spend a lot of time alone and on your own. You control your time, you choose what you get to work on, and you are responsible for doing the work the way that works best for you. The bad news is that you have to make good choices and get the work done even when you're unmotivated or you aren't sure what you should be working on, and some days you don't even know how to begin tackling all those tasks in front of you.

To be effective as a remote teammate:

- You need to get your work done so they continue to pay you.

- You need to be able to plan your work effectively.

- You need to be able to prioritize tasks that match what your team requires.

- You need to build solid relationships with your coworkers and manager to ensure work gets done.

- You need to avoid distractions.

■ You need to adjust your communication style and behavior to the fact that you're not face-to-face.

■ You need to motivate yourself on days when you're just not feeling it.

In this part, we'll start with a model that will help you with every part of your life as a remote worker. Then we'll look at the mindset it takes to be a great remote teammate. After that we will get super practical—addressing some of the challenges you face every day: how to stay motivated, manage your time and productivity, and build routines that will support your success.

Chapter 1

The 3P Model for Remote-Work Success

Alice has worked in the main office for five years and has great relationships with her coworkers, her manager, and people throughout the organization. Six months ago, she moved to another city and was able to retain her position. Everything was going great—until lately.

While she began working with people she knew, there have since been additions to the team. She doesn't know these people as well and doesn't go to them for assistance like she does her long-time colleagues. Last week, a new project was announced, and for the first time, she wasn't approached about being part of the team. More than that, it seems there are more meetings than ever, and they seem to accomplish less. As a remote team member, she doesn't know when to give her input—or if it is even wanted.

Even though she is doing her job, she feels less motivated to go the extra mile than she used to. She told a friend, "I'm just not as connected to the job as I used to be."

What Alice is going through is not unusual. When we begin working remotely, we are often energized. No commute! We can work in our Led Zeppelin T-shirt! We can take the kids to school and get so much more done when they're not there!

Over time, though, studies show that our productivity, the quality of our relationships, and our overall engagement may begin to decline. Some of that is the natural result of the novelty of a welcome situation wearing off. After the honeymoon phase, you're left with the day-to-day reality of working without regular social interaction, knowing what is going on, or having access to the boss or your coworkers whenever you want it.

In working with managers and remote workers around the world, we have spent a lot of time asking what makes someone successful when they work apart from everyone else. This was a trickier question than we thought, because what does it mean to be successful?

- Is success getting your work done every day? Does it stop there?

- Does success mean you are getting promoted regularly?

- Does success mean you are satisfied with your work-life balance?

- Do you have satisfying work relationships that make your day enjoyable?

There are almost as many definitions of success as there are people. So we asked ourselves, Is there a common thread among workers who, regardless of the work they do, are engaged, productive, and satisfied with their work?

There is.

The 3P Model of Remote-Work Success

We have identified three factors that impact the overall quality of remote work. Three areas that, if you give them the attention they deserve, can greatly enhance the quality of your work, enhance your relationships with others, and help you create the kind of workplace and long-term success you desire, even when you don't work in the company's headquarters or right under your boss's nose.

This model introduces the concept of the *3Ps* (see figure 1). Here's our definition of each factor:

Productivity

Not surprisingly, "Productivity" is the top of the model. That seems simple enough. After all, getting the job done is typically the prime factor in whether you keep a job, regardless of where you work. This is the question most organizations ask themselves when considering remote work: Will we get at least as much quality work from someone if they don't work alongside everyone else?

Figure 1. The 3P Model

If you started working from home so you could get work done without constant interruptions and the day-to-day craziness of the office, this might seem like a no-brainer. But getting tasks accomplished is not the same as being productive.

By definition, productivity is the measure of work yielding results, benefits, or profits. It is about outcomes, not activity. So while it isn't unusual for remote workers to be busy, the question isn't so much "Are you working?" as "What are you working on?" "How's it going?" and "What does it bring to the team's goals and outcomes?"

A *team member* focuses on their work and tasks. A *teammate* considers not only how to be personally productive to get the most and best work done in the time allotted, but how to help the rest of the team and organization meet its goals.

You probably know that remote workers work plenty of hours. But working hard and putting in lots of hours isn't the same as being productive. Face it, your work is always within arm's reach and calling your name. It's hard to disconnect. You hear, or say, things like:

- I'll just work a little bit more after the kids go to bed.

- Instead of watching TV tonight, I'll just catch up on my email.

At the end of the day, real productivity is about getting more of the right or best things done—not how much time you spent doing it.

In the rest of the book we'll examine the mindset, skills, and habits we can develop to help us maintain our productivity, even when we're uninspired, uncertain of what we're doing, or just plain exhausted.

Proactivity

Perhaps the most surprising thing we uncovered in our research was the one word that both managers and workers agreed best described a great remote teammate. That word was *proactivity*.

The technical definition of the word *proactive* is "acting in anticipation of future problems, needs, or changes."[1] Translated to our work, that means thinking longer term and bigger picture. Being *proactive* is the opposite of being *reactive*.

Here's a simple example. The best and safest drivers are proactive by looking further down the road. They notice what's right in front of them while adjusting to what is further ahead. They drive straighter, drive more smoothly, and are far safer. Reactive drivers are looking barely past the hood of their vehicle. A ride with them will be far less enjoyable, jerkier, and likely less safe.

It makes sense that managers want team members who think bigger and into the future. Proactive teammates don't wait to be told what to do and ask the questions that could help them be more productive. But there are several not-so-obvious ways that proactivity is especially valuable when working remotely.

When we think of someone being proactive, we usually think of the motto "If you see something, say something." A good teammate will offer suggestions if a colleague is struggling. They'll speak up in a meeting if a point needs to be made. If a task must be completed, they will offer to help. That behavior is obvious and highly valued.

But when we dug behind the answers, we found a different form of proactivity that was neither as obvious nor as common. It isn't just about tasks, it's also about your mindset.

When you have a question about your work, do you ask for clarification immediately or do you just try to work through it? In coaching conversations, do you accept that your manager isn't talking about your personal development plan or do you raise the subject yourself? When that meeting is running long, do you speak up and try to get the team back on track or do you sit back, roll your eyes, and go answer your email instead?

Both managers and team members say that the thing they look for most in a teammate is that kind of initiative. It requires bravery, trust, and engagement but may be the single most important component in your long-term success as a remote worker.

Potential

Finally, do you consider the long-term implications of your work and the choices you make? This is perhaps the most difficult thing about working remotely, and often contributes to our feelings of isolation and disengagement over time.

By putting your head down and focusing on your own work, have you taken yourself off your manager's radar for future assignments?

Perhaps you are so focused on completing an assignment that you have appeared rude or pushy to others. Have you considered what that snippy email might mean in the future, or is accomplishing this task right now the only thing on your mind?

When you are in the middle of something, and just trying to get the job done and move on, it's easy to forget that short-term decisions can have long-term impacts.

For your teammates, one inconsiderate moment might not matter, but if it becomes a pattern, it will certainly change how they think of you.

Your manager is looking at your behavior, decision making, and engagement over a longer time frame than just this one task or project. If you take a pass on this assignment or don't participate in a particular discussion, what will it mean for future interactions and opportunities?

What is your goal for this job in the short term? What do you want to accomplish here? How do you feel you can make the biggest contribution, and what are your goals long term? Does it help you build the skills and experience you desire? And how does this role fit into your vision for yourself?

Many of us spend too little time thinking about this, and yet it is important to your long-term engagement, job satisfaction, and career goals. If it's so critical, why don't we think and talk about it more often?

Everything we do has both immediate and long-term impact. Are you focused on the immediate need, or do you consider the potential results of your activities, behavior, and communication style?

Let's look at three examples:

- *Office politics.* It's not uncommon when we work away from the office to be blissfully unaware of what's going on in the workplace, smugly believing that we are above or immune to office politics. But is the fact that you are not aware of upcoming decisions or haven't built relationships with decision makers part of the reason you seem stalled at your current position?

- *Transactional communication.* One of the traps when we work remotely is a tendency for our work, our communication, and our planning to become very transactional. We need to finish this task, and we're not overly concerned if Bob in Accounting likes it—at least until we need a favor from Bob. Are you taking the time to tend to the relationship and create some friendly interaction or are you focusing completely on the transactional work?

- *Tuning out in meetings.* Meetings can seem like an interruption to our work. It's a hassle to contribute when the people in the conference room are always dominating the conversation anyway. If we tune out, we can't be surprised that people don't seek our input or consider us interested. If the people in the office don't know what we bring to the party, why should they even invite us?

Thinking long term and about your potential isn't natural and doesn't come easily when you're extinguishing the latest fire or just trying to get that task done and off your list.

You're already working away from others. If you consider productivity, proactivity, and potential, odds are you'll be more than a remote worker, you'll be a great teammate and member of the organization.

Pause and Reflect

▶ Overall, how productive do you feel you are most days?

▶ How happy are you with your proactivity? (How would your peers answer that question about you?)

▶ Who would you identify as a role model for proactivity that you could learn from?

▶ How often do you think about your potential in your work and career? Is it enough?

Online Resource

For an activity to help you apply the 3P Model for yourself in your work now, register at the website:

LongDistanceTeammate.com/resources

and request the **3P Model Activity**.

Chapter 2

Getting Your Mindset Right

José was comfortable working in the office. He knew what worked, what to do, and how to get things done. More than comfortable, he was successful. All the feedback he received supported the fact that he was valued and was doing well. Now that he is moving to work from home because of a reorganization, he wonders what will change. His job description hasn't changed, but he wonders how much different things will really be. Amid this change, mostly he wonders if how he thinks about his role and work must change too.

One of the reasons you are reading this book is that you want to be more comfortable and successful as a remote worker. We don't know your background—whether, like José, you are preparing for or have just started working remotely or are an old hand at it. Perhaps you are struggling and need some tips, or maybe you have been working remotely for some time and just want to improve.

Beyond your comfort, experience, and success levels, your working situations vary as well. We are aware that you might not be working from home as a full-time dedicated resource to the organization who pays you. You might better describe your work situation as one of the following:

- *I'm a gig worker.* I'm just picking up some cash or some experience, and I'm working from home to do it.

- *I'm a project worker.* When this project is over, I'm on to the next thing.

- *I'm a contractor.* I do similar work as the rest of the team, but my job status isn't as an employee, so I might not be a permanent member of the organization.

- *I'm a short-timer.* I don't see this as my long-term job.

Before we get into the skills, tactics, and techniques that will help you succeed, we must start with your mindset. We want you to understand your current viewpoint about work, specifically when working away from others, and then we will propose a mindset that we know will help you be more successful.

This proposed way of thinking applies regardless of your personal situation, as we have already described. In the previous chapter where we outlined the 3P Model of remote-work success, we started developing the mindset we recommend. In this chapter we will be more specific, challenging you to consider how you think about your work and work situation, and depending on your current mindset, boldly suggesting something different and better.

While this book will help you tactically (both personally and as a part of the team) in the short term, for it to be most helpful to you, we hope it changes your mindset, and not just your skills.

Having said that, let's get started.

It's Not Just Your Job, It's Your Career

Every day matters.

You may be here thinking about the short term. How to succeed (or even just survive) in your current working situation. It doesn't matter how you got here. It doesn't matter what the current work or role is, whether this is just a short-term job or gig to help pay for college, or if you don't plan to do this kind of work for long. The work may not connect to the work you love or plan, but the way you think about this job today and the way you do the work will have an impact on your long-term success. Every day you work you build habits and routines. And, like any other habit, the longer you do things in one way, the harder it will be to change your behavior later.

While you may be thinking about all of this with a short-term view, there's more to it than that. This is about your career, and your entire life. We want you to be thinking about what success—both today and tomorrow—looks like to you. It might always include working remotely; it might not. Beyond the daily work, be thinking about how every day now is contributing to the career that you want to create.

Here's another way to think differently about your future. Everything in this book will apply to you for the rest of your career, even as your role evolves. Remote work isn't going away, even if you aren't the one doing it. Perhaps sooner rather than later you may work in the office or on-site with other people. Even then, the odds are you will still have others on your team who are remote or you're going to be leading others who work remotely. This chapter will help you view your work in ways that will always serve you.

One more thing—one of the challenges of working remotely is wondering if you will be seen and be able to be promoted if you aren't in the office. We'll talk about lots of ways to deal with those concerns and succeed. It must start with thinking beyond this job to your whole career.

It's Not Just Your Job, It's about Organizational Success

Why are you doing the job?

There are a bunch of personal reasons, including the following:

- You need to eat.

- You know you are supposed to work.

- You are tired of daytime TV.

- It keeps you out of mischief.

While these may be accurate, none of them matter to the organization who is giving you money in return for your efforts. You are a part of an organization. You have been hired one way or another to help create great results for that entity. And so, it is in your best interest to think about your work (and it may be harder when you don't walk into an office with the organization's name on the door) from the perspective of the organization. This is particularly true if you're not a full-time employee. You're not just doing the daily work—to be most successful, you must think about that daily work in the context of what you bring, not just what you take home every two weeks.

Your success is defined more broadly than finishing the work you've been given. Your success must be tied to organizational success.

It's Not Just Your Job, You're Part of a Team

As a remote team member, you can easily forget this. When we work away from others on our team, it can be hard to see a picture of our work that's beyond what we see right around us. That's one reason why it is easy to forget that we're a part of a larger group. But just because you might feel alone, or like you're fending for yourself, doesn't make it true. A critical part of your ultimate success is recognizing your role on the team and making it part of your work every day.

Here's how we describe it:

Your job = your work + team work

Mine and ours; your job consists of both. First you must recognize that reality, then you need to understand how to balance each in the course of your daily activities. Let's use this picture to help us discuss it (see figure 2).

The "Your Work" Box

The "your work" box consists of the stuff that you are already (or need to be) doing. Hopefully, you are doing all this well, and even if you're not, you likely know most of what is in this box. It is another way of stating your key job responsibilities. These are the things you are measured against, that you have benchmarks for. Perhaps it is your KPIs. This is the stuff in your job description, although most job descriptions are a little too high level.

This box is what most people think about their job as, and how they would describe it to a semi-interested person at a cocktail party. It's the technical process part of the work, the stuff you probably do as an individual and what you would say you were hired to do. This is what is on your task list and it's what you are working on. If you split your time between home and the office, you get most of this done when you are alone. That might be why you chose to be out of the office—so you can get more of it done.

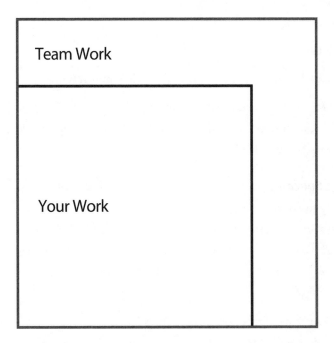

Figure 2. A full picture of your work

It's possible the "your work" box is all you think about. It's the most concrete way to look at your work, and because you're working remotely, it's quite possibly too insular and too siloed. If you are thinking "That sounds fine to me," you are thinking incorrectly.

The "Team Work" Box

The items in the "team work" box are outside of yourself. They include a lot of the things we will help you think about in this book. Anytime you are engaging with the rest of the team, or other people on the team, you are operating in this box.

Here is a general list:

- Building relationships

- Building trust

- Effectively communicating

- Collaborating

- Mentoring

- Participating in meetings, projects, and other joint activities

When you are working with a bigger picture perspective, and are doing things in relationship to the larger work of the team and organization, you are working in the "team work" box.

Getting Specific

It is easy to conceptualize our point, and even agree with it. But a general idea isn't enough. How do you determine the specific details of what is in your "team work" box? Because this is work outside of your immediate view, you need to ask others—both your leader and your teammates—what they need:

- *Your leader.* Make sure you know their expectations of you. How would they describe what they need from you, beyond the core work? Find out what your success looks like from their perspective and how you can support their goals for the team.

- *Your teammates.* Your teammates are your peers, but also likely your internal customers too. What do they want or need from you? How can you help them reach their goals? How can you make work easier and more productive for them? Their expectations matter because you're all in this work together.

So, the "team work" box includes the expectations and needs of your boss and teammates. Is there anything else?

It's also your awareness of a bigger picture out there that you are not only a part of but have a responsibility for. It's your alignment with organizational goals. It's recognizing how what you do connects with what the team needs to do and how that's connected with the organization. It's a line-of-sight issue. Can you see how what you do connects with the team's work? Does it tie to what the organization needs? When you have that picture of that alignment, you quickly see that your job is bigger than just "your work" and, in fact,

Your job = your work + team work

The teammate mindset starts with clearer expectations—both from others and of yourself. Until you see your work in this way, you can never have the kind of success and impact that is possible.

We know, we just expanded your job. Once you have this mindset, the question becomes—How do I balance all the work? You'll need to be able to:

- Recognize a balance is needed

- Get clarity and feedback from others

- Set your own time boundaries (personal and professional too!)

- Determine how much time to spend on each box

- Be comfortable with the blur between the boxes

- Remain aware—reflect and adjust

Don't worry, we will address all these things throughout the book.

Your Engagement Matters—And Belongs to You

We mentioned this in the introduction, but it is important enough to say again. (Plus, some people skip the introduction. If you did, it is worth going back to it now.) How engaged you are in your work is important. It matters to your performance. It determines how you feel about your work and can make it bearable or keep you inspired even on the hard days when you feel isolated or like a lone wolf. It matters to how others see you and how valuable you are to the greater effort of the organization.

And engagement is your choice. It isn't something to wait for senior leadership or your boss to do. It isn't as simple as the idea that you can't be engaged because you don't get to go to happy hour with the rest of the team. Being an engaged teammate starts, and largely ends, with you. We believe this mindset will greatly aid your success, contentment, and happiness. The good news is, as you adopt the other mindsets and habits in this chapter, this one will make more sense and likely become the way you see the world.

Final Thoughts

You have mindsets—beliefs about your work and working situation that are guiding you now. We strongly urge you to examine these. How does your current set of thoughts and beliefs impact your work, relationships, and overall motivation and energy? All the skills, approaches, and ideas that follow will be most effective and easier to implement and maintain when backed by a teammate mindset.

Pause and Reflect

▶ When you think about your work, how successfully do you consider your teammates and the organization as well as your own work?

▶ How well do you strike a balance between your tasks and the team's work?

Online Resource

For a process to help you identify the specific items in your "team work" box, register at the website:

LongDistanceTeammate.com/resources

and request the **Team Work Tool**.

Chapter 3

Getting and Staying Motivated When You Work Alone

Susan really enjoys working away from the office. She feels productive and doesn't miss the endless get-togethers, birthday cake in the break room, and people popping over her cubicle wall to chit-chat. That isolation of working remotely used to energize her, and she would get more done on most days than she ever did in the office. Some days, though, she finds it hard to do more than the bare minimum. Work is still getting done, but she doesn't seem to have the energy or excitement about the work she used to have.

The good news about working at a distance is that you can (within reason) set your own pace, work on what you need to work on when you are at your best, and not be interrupted by silly questions and unimportant conversations. When you're on your game, you are super-productive, and everyone knows it. You feed on the raw power of accomplishment and self-worth.

Then there are the other days.

Maybe you look at your to-do list and think, "Ugh. Why bother? Nobody notices anyway." Maybe no matter how busy you are, your task list never seems to shrink. Or it seems you haven't spoken to another human being in days. Whatever it is, you can't seem to shake off the funk. When you feel this way, it can be hard to do good work, and there's nobody around to help you get past those feelings.

It's also easy to believe that you are the only one who feels this way. Your email in-box tells you everyone else seems to be working at full speed, and you're only getting further behind, which does nothing for your mood.

The truth is you are not alone.

The next time you aren't as motivated or energized as you feel you should be, remember: even the highest performers in every field you can think of have had days when their energy, focus, or desire to get out of bed is lower than other times. It's natural. It's temporary, and (unless it goes on for too long) it's seldom career limiting. You'll probably snap out of it.

But we are here to give you tools to snap out of it faster and be in that lull state for shorter periods of time.

Most of us get over this feeling quickly. It takes only one good phone call, or a breakthrough idea that has you breezing through that report in no time, or just a particularly good cup of tea. That's great, but it's not much comfort in the meantime.

Think about your cell phone as an example (or don't; for many of us that's part of our demotivation). Whether it's plugged in or running on battery power, it works the same way. For a while. Eventually, though, if your phone is not plugged in, that little battery symbol will become emptier and emptier until the phone stops working entirely.

That's us. We are self-governing, independent, capable people. But without the information, human contact, and energy of being "plugged in" with the rest of our team, we eventually fade and become less effective.

There are many reasons we become demotivated. Here is a partial list:

- Being bored

- Experiencing a lack of progress on important projects

- Dealing with unpleasant coworkers

- Missing the energy of others

- Feeling unappreciated for our work

- Believing we're being micromanaged or overworked

- Receiving little positive feedback on our work

- Feeling unable to meet the needs of those in our personal life (our spouse, the kids, and even the dog)

- Getting sucked into the news, even if the TV *should* be off

- Being physically or mentally depleted

You could probably add half a dozen items to this list with no problem, and that can feel overwhelming and a bit demotivating, which pretty much defeats the purpose of this chapter.

Do you notice how some of these are the exact opposite of another? A lot of that has to do with your work style and personality. If you get energy from interacting with others, not talking to people is like forgetting to plug in your charger. If you prefer to be alone, maybe you need to put your communication technologies on "Do Not Disturb" for a bit. Nothing works the same for every person, and it may even vary from day to day.

Regardless of your particular list of causes, once we realize that a momentary feeling of ennui (which is a fancy way of saying restlessness) or dissatisfaction is normal, we also know that the reasons fall into a few easily identified categories. We feel like we're lacking:

- Energy

- Focus

- Purpose

- Useful feedback

Unless your feelings about your job are irreparable, positively adjusting any one of these factors might be exactly what you need to get back on track.

Addressing a Lack of Energy

When talking about the energy to get work done, it could be physical or mental energy or, more often, a combination of both. Working separately from other people often results in doing tasks in ways that might feel right, but often are counterproductive in the long run.

People who work from home report that they work longer hours than those who go to the office. That's not because we're better people (okay, maybe a little bit), but it's for a variety of other factors, depending on the specifics of your job:

■ *No commute.* Without the logistical challenges of getting to work, we have more time to work.

■ *No barriers.* We start as soon as we get up and get through our morning routine (or even before that) and often don't stop when everyone else does, because we are always around our work.

■ *Work is always there.* We see it and we're trained to respond. It's harder than ever to escape.

■ *There's something to prove.* Maybe we are trying to prove to our coworkers and our employer that we are working hard when they're not watching.

One way to keep your energy level up is to not drain yourself. Work with your manager to meet the requirements of the job. Set a realistic, and agreed to, start and stop time for your work and then walk away. Shut down your computer or close your office door when it's quitting time. If you don't have a door, at least shut down that laptop.

We know the laptop isn't the whole problem, though. Chances are you are carrying a tether to your work 24/7. It is called your phone. Make sure you set boundaries on how much you will allow yourself to engage with work from your phone during nonworking hours. Turning off the email notification is a good first step. Manage your screen time no matter what device it is.

Another way we drain energy is by not taking breaks during the day. For whatever reason, whether it's paranoia, hyperfocus, or dedication to our work, we often don't schedule and take breaks the way we do when working in the office. Even when we stop working, we then switch over to our favorite social media destination or watch YouTube, but we are still sitting at the same desk, staring at the same screen, and sitting on our same backside.

Here are some tips for keeping your energy level high:

■ *Take a break.* For every forty to sixty minutes of uninterrupted work, you should take ten minutes to get up, stretch, walk around the house, get something done, look out the window, and then get back to work.

- *Eat healthier.* The fact that you're at home should make this easier. Avoid sugars and heavy starches (especially if you're not going to take breaks), and once your morning coffee has been consumed, avoid caffeine-heavy drinks.

- *Get physical.* Use some of that time you aren't working to get some physical activity. Exercise doesn't have to mean getting on a bike and SoulCycling yourself into a coma unless that's your idea of fun. Simply go for a walk with the dog or a friend, park farther from the store, or go to the gym. Play with your children. Even household chores can get the blood going. Anything that isn't sitting and staring at a screen will help.

- *Talk to someone pleasant.* When you are dealing with a constant stream of negative energy, talking to someone might feel like the last thing you want to do. But positive energy is infectious, and talking to someone who has energy to spare often works out well for both parties. It doesn't even have to be work related, although that certainly helps ease the guilt, if that's part of your self-talk.

People who work in different time zones from their employer often struggle with this, since the time most people take (before work or after work) is often the very time you need to be functional. Your company may have specific times or needs for you to be available depending on the work you do. Take that into consideration.

Wayne works on the West Coast in the Pacific time zone, while most of his colleagues and many clients are on Eastern time. The three hour difference means that the early mornings, which used to be gym time, are now filled with conference calls and urgent Slack messages. For you, it may mean moving gym time to the afternoon, or simply blocking a quiet time during the day to get that walk in.

Addressing a Lack of Focus

What can you do on those days when you feel overwhelmed, or bored with what you're doing, or just plain unable to concentrate?

The most effective way to reengage is simply to stop whatever you're doing and ask yourself, "What has my attention right now, and is it what I *should* pay attention to?"

If you're not working on what you think you should be, what are you thinking about? Odds are it won't take a lot to get yourself refocused; here are some suggestions. And, yes, some will sound easier than they are.

- *Stop what you're doing.* Seriously. Knock it off. Your brain might just need to refocus. One of the big mistakes we make when working on projects and tasks that we know will take time (like writing chapters in books!) is that we believe we are able to focus for longer than we really can. Our brains are capable of high attention and focus for only thirty to forty minutes at a time. That's why even if we've blocked an hour to do something, we are really operating at peak efficiency for only a portion of that. If you are working on something really time consuming, you might find you get more done in three half-hour blocks than in ninety minutes of sitting staring at a screen. Your brain is wandering because it needs a break.

- *Eliminate the mental distractions.* Are you trying to finish that report but you can't get your mind off that email you owe Bob, or the sink full of dishes? Rather than trying to power through, you might be better off just taking the time to get those off your plate so that your brain can get back to business. Those tasks usually take far less time to accomplish than they take out of your productivity just worrying about them.

- *Eliminate the physical distractions.* These can be nonwork temptations like your phone, or web surfing, or sounds and visual distractions. Try physically putting your distractions out of reach like charging your phone across the room or putting it in a bottom drawer while you are working on something requiring your full attention. One of the easiest productivity enhancers is to turn off the incoming email and message notifications. They will still show up in your in-box but won't interrupt the flow of your work. Block time when you'll deal with email, so it doesn't distract you. Closing your web browser when working on another application is surprisingly effective, even if you go through withdrawal the first time or two.

- *Create a work rhythm.* Schedule your work by alternating high-focus, high-value work with all the administrative things that take up your mental bandwidth. That way you can get those smaller tasks accomplished quickly without feeling guilty, while allowing yourself to focus on the high-value work for more intense periods. It's surprising how the positive feeling of checking things off your list gives you the ability to slow down and focus afterward.

- *Confirm priorities.* Make sure that what you're focusing on is most important. Check your assumptions with others about the timeline for the work you are struggling with. Perhaps you can come back to it in the morning when you're fresh, or after dinner when you get your second wind.

- *Use your power hours.* If your role allows flexibility in when you do your work, consider when you are at your best. While we aren't suggesting working more hours, if a midday trip to the gym, followed by working until seven, works better for you—and fits the job—do it.

Addressing a Lack of Purpose

The most obvious sign that you lack motivation is asking yourself the question, "Who cares?" Does it feel like your work is going unappreciated, so it's not worth trying so hard? Maybe you feel like your work isn't important to the team's goals. On your worst days you wonder why you should put in an effort when it doesn't seem like anyone else is.

You do your best work when seeing the bigger picture, when you have a sense of purpose, believe the work is important, and know that your best efforts make a difference. When you are struggling, you can end up in a mental tailspin that is hard to pull out of by yourself. What's needed is a fresh perspective and possibly some evidence that you're on track.

When feeling a lack of purpose:

- *Remember the why.* Reexamine the real reason you're doing this work. Take a moment to reread your project charter or team values statement. Does it ring true? Go back and ask yourself, How does the menial, boring task I'm doing impact people down the line? Most of us don't care if a Form 26-B gets completed, but we do want to make sure Tom gets paid, which is what that form will ensure.

- *Look for progress.* Check your team's metrics, dashboard, and project status. Sometimes we need to see the big picture in order to appreciate the little things. It's likely you've made more progress than you think, or you are a bit behind and just seeing is enough to kick you into a higher gear.

- *Talk to a customer (internal or external) and get a quick "win."* Hearing the positive reaction of another human being to our efforts is energizing.

One of the biggest reasons we feel a temporary lack of purpose is that we lack the information to know whether we're making a difference or not. That leads us to the last factor, feedback.

Addressing a Lack of Feedback

Feedback is important to the quality of our work. It's also critical for our mental well-being. Without knowing that our work is done well, is on time, and is appreciated, we are drawing completely on internal resources that drain quickly. On our best days we are positive, confident in our abilities, and rulers of our world. On bad days, though, if the only voices we hear are the ones in our own heads saying, "This is really awful," or "Why bother? Nobody's going to appreciate my hard work anyway," it is hard to maintain a positive attitude.

The problem with feedback is that it requires communicating with other people. This is where understanding your work style and those of others and being proactive are particularly important.

Seek input from your teammates. If there are people who depend on you for input, it's within reason to ensure they are getting what they need. Regardless of how well you know Tom, it is perfectly valid to ask if that work you sent him was correct, and if there's anything else you need to know. Odds are, he'll respond with a positive, supportive message and that will help eliminate that negative self-talk. If there is something you could do better, it might help explain the nagging feeling you're having, and set you off on a new, focused direction. Odds are you have people on the team that you trust and enjoy working with more than others. It doesn't hurt to start with them! It might even add some fun to your day, which goes a long way toward banishing those black clouds hanging over your head.

Seek input and feedback from your manager. This can often feel uncomfortable, but they are charged with giving you feedback on a regular basis. Most leaders know they should give you feedback more regularly, especially because you work remotely, but for whatever reason, they don't do it. By asking, you give them a chance to talk about the quality and importance of your job, and you are helping them and likely strengthening your relationship. Approach it from a place of work, as opposed to your attitude. "I want to make sure that I'm working on this the right way" is better than "I am working in a black hole of silence and just need to know I'm not alone in the world."

We will talk much more about feedback in chapter 11, including how to both give it to and receive it from teammates and your manager, but for now, this should be enough to help re-motivate you on the days you need it.

Pause and Reflect

► What is your energy and motivation level most days? Are you happy with that answer?

► What blocks and drains your energy and motivation?

► What maintains or builds your energy and motivation?

Chapter 4

Getting (the Right) Stuff Done

Cassie is working from home more often than ever before. While she has a desk in the office, she finds that the commute is hard on her and she prefers to work uninterrupted. At first, she found she got more checked off her task list at home. Recently, though, she's feeling like she's putting in more hours and still not accomplishing what she used to. Email interruptions and meetings are cutting into time she should be "working." Most days things are fine, but sometimes the frustration can be overwhelming.

When we ask people why they enjoy working from home or away from the office (aside from losing the commute), often the answer is "I can get more done." Studies bear this out.[1] People who work away from the office often check more tasks off their to-do list than when they are interrupted by coworkers or there is yet another birthday cake in the break room.

For the most part, this task-focused productivity is a good thing. After all, it's the reason we're hired. It's the first question senior leadership asks about those who work remotely: Are they working and how do we know? In our surveys, the people who know you best (your manager and your peers) don't worry about this so much. In most cases, they know you're working.

But working hard and putting in time at your desk is not the same as being productive. Many teleworkers report that while we put in the time, we often feel like we aren't making the progress we should. The freedom to set our own schedule also means we often don't manage our time. This can lead many to put in more time than those who commute to the office. Some of the most common complaints are:

- We get more done because we work longer hours than we should. Our days start as soon as we roll out of bed (and some are checking email while still under the covers!) and often don't end until we are back in bed.

- We find ourselves focusing on individual tasks rather than team project work that might be more valuable. This balance between "team work" and our personal tasks is one of the hardest things to achieve, and we'll talk about it more in the next chapter.

- The benefit of being away from the office seems to have vanished. We're interrupted by emails, texts, IMs, and phone calls as much as we were when we worked with everyone else.

- Some days it's difficult to make a dent in our growing task list and we are so busy "putting out fires" that we can't make progress on the truly important things we need to do.

- We are so determined to prove that we can be trusted to get our work done that we don't seek help or guidance when we should, meaning we often dig ourselves a hole, and it takes time and energy to climb out. This makes the "I'll just work more hours" rabbit hole deeper as well.

Being productive and being busy aren't the same thing. In our 3P Model, we stressed that Productivity is doing the right work in the right amount of time for both your benefit and that of your teammates. That seems like it should be simple enough, so why do we sometimes feel overwhelmed, burned out, and like we've lost whatever control we were supposed to gain by working remotely?

As Kevin has been pointing out for years, what we call time management is really choice management—it is about the choices we make with the time we have. Everyone has the same number of minutes, hours, and days in the workweek. Why do some people seem to get things done in the time allotted and others struggle?

When you have other people around, you sometimes draw inspiration or energy from them. When you are alone, you may feel drained and confused about what you should be working on and when. How can you catch yourself and change course before you get discouraged and frustrated?

Most days you know what you're doing: you have a list and you tackle it. Other days, not so much, and the frustration mounts. It doesn't have to be that way.

The Four Pivot Questions

We suggest you ask yourself these four questions when you are snowed under with work, or staring at your task list, convinced that you'll never make a dent. We call them "pivot questions," because when you get the answers, they can help you change direction and make real progress.

The four pivot questions are:

- Where is your focus right now?

- What is the best use of your time?

- How can you influence others to maximize your productivity?

- What habits impact your productivity and results?

Where Is Your Focus Right Now?

In a perfect world, we choose a task, work on it until it's done, and then move on to the next job. In the real world, it doesn't often happen that way. You begin building that presentation, and you get an incoming email. It might be important, so you stop, read it, answer it, and then get back to your work only to get a panicky instant message from a teammate. We convince ourselves that we are being productive because we are multitasking, trying to do many jobs at once.

There's only one problem: multitasking is a myth.

The human brain is a single-task processor. When we do more than one thing at a time, we aren't doing them simultaneously. We actually switch back and forth from one task to the other. When we're bouncing around like that, our brains can't give 100 percent attention to any of the jobs we're juggling.

In fact, if you are constantly interrupted by distractions like email, you may be working at a maximum of only 70 percent of your capacity.[2] The seductive thing about this is some of the time that's enough. When you're clearing out your in-box, or performing mindless administrative tasks, you might not need to be at your absolute best, and you can check-check-check things off your list.

But when we get in the habit of responding to interruptions, like when email becomes a productivity killer instead of a tool, or instant messages take us away from higher-value work, we need to stop and think about where our brains are focusing.

On a gut level, you probably know this. But why do smart people allow themselves to get so distracted?

In part, this is because you want to be seen as a responsive teammate. Or it could be important to you that your boss knows you are at your desk working, so the faster you respond the better. Sometimes you feel so isolated that any chance to talk to or interact with another human being overtakes the need to finish whatever you're working on.

Whatever the reason, if distractions are stopping you from accomplishing what's important, there are some steps you can take:

- *Identify and remove the distraction.* If you are constantly reaching for your cell phone (and the average office worker looks at their phone at least 150 times a day[3]), place it out of your line of sight, and preferably out of reach so it takes effort to look at it.

  While you might not be able to stop checking email and IMs completely, turning off the audible "dings" and "beeps" that capture your attention and force you to respond like Pavlov's dogs, salivating at every bell, is a heck of a start. When you make this recommended change, it may lead you to resetting expectations with others. There is more about this in chapter 12.

- *Structure your time to allow full concentration.* While we recommend turning off your email and other notifications, that might not be possible in your role. And even when it is possible, people have often told us how stressful it is to ignore the messages that they "know" are piling up. Believe us, you can: assign specific times to check messages. Start with fifteen- or thirty-minute intervals. You might be able to work up to an hour or more. Then check in every hour or so. You'll be surprised what a difference it makes in your productivity.

If it makes you feel any better, studies show that our brain can only maintain "peak focus" for thirty-five to forty-five minutes at a time. You'll get better results by focusing on one important thing until you're out of steam, then switching to something else. The good news is that very often you're free to choose the blocks of time you assign to which projects.

■ *Beware of shiny objects.* The hard truth is that most of what pulls our attention, whatever the new thing is, is likely more interesting than what we're working on. Depending on the day, it might be something you find more fun to do, a chance to connect with a teammate, or just responding to anything your manager asks you to do. Before jumping at it, ask yourself, Is this where I should be focused right now?

What Is the Best Use of Your Time?

It might seem like a blessing to be left alone to decide what you should be working on and when. But sometimes your brain begins to second-guess yourself: Are you balancing all the work (including stuff beyond what is on your immediate task list)? Which of the four things your manager asked you to do is the top priority now? Is this important to you but will it negatively impact someone else's job?

Setting priorities can be difficult when left to our own devices. Sometimes it's because you get conflicting advice or requests from other people. Sometimes it's the voices in your head arguing about what should be done when, and occasionally you have so much on your plate you don't know where to start.

Here are some guidelines for setting your priorities:

■ *Think big picture.* When you stare at a to-do list, it's easy to take each task at face value and treat them all equally. This is especially true the more panicked and frustrated you are. Take a deep breath and ask yourself where this particular task fits into the bigger picture of the organization and your team's needs.

When you're struggling to prioritize tasks, it helps to look at the nonnegotiable factors. Things like hard deadlines, for example, can help clarify your next order of business. Account for your deadlines, and those of your teammates and the project team or organization. If others can't get their work done until you do something first, move that up your priority list. The feeling of accomplishment from helping the team might spill over into the energy needed to tackle something on your personal list.

■ *Be realistic about "important" versus "urgent."* When you're looking at a growing task list, it is tempting to tackle the easy things—the jobs you can check off the list fastest—first. That means you are busy, but are you accomplishing anything important? While there is some satisfaction to crossing something off, those items often aren't what need to be done the most.

While you're probably familiar with the concept of "important versus urgent," it's worth a reminder that "knowing" something and "doing it" are not always the same thing. *Urgent* tasks are the things that feel as though they demand our immediate attention. Sometimes they do, like when there is a hard and fast deadline assigned to them. Other times, they can feel critical (requests for assistance from peers, or when your manager asks if you can do something for them that might pull you away from more important tasks, but they're THE BOSS).

Important tasks have long-reaching impacts on you, your team, and the project or organization. They fit firmly under the "Potential" part of the 3P Model. Ask yourself, If this task doesn't get done, what is the long-term impact? And how will things be improved when this is successfully completed?

■ *Break the elephant into bite-sized pieces.* There's an old riddle that goes, "How do you eat a whole elephant? One bite at a time." (Nobody said it was funny, just true.) Sometimes you look at a task or project and it is overwhelming. Why start, when you know you will have only twenty minutes or so before the next interruption? Sometimes the answer is to look at that elephant and break it into manageable chunks. You might not get that report written, but you can get your research organized. Maybe you can't solve that customer problem entirely, but you can alert the other stakeholders and schedule that meeting. Nobody says you have to do it all at once, and most projects can be handled as a series of small, easily managed pieces.

- *Check with others if you have conflicting priorities or can't decide.* This is one of those "proactivity" things that many good remote teammates don't do perhaps out of fear that they will look foolish. It isn't a sign of weakness or failure to ask your manager which of the four things they've given you to do takes priority. Find out what your teammates are working on (and why) or what they most need from you right now. If the priority isn't obvious, sometimes we can be paralyzed by the number of choices. When that happens, get some help in deciding. Trust us, your manager and teammates would much prefer you get their opinion than have you working on things that don't make their lives easier.

How Can You Influence Others to Maximize Your Productivity?

We've said that interruptions are a problem for our productivity. Have you ever wondered why interruptions occur?

Sure, people can be inconsiderate. And yes, the universe doesn't care about what you planned today. But one of the major contributors to lost production is the way we've taught others to work with us.

Wait. What?

Think about it this way. If every time someone asks a question in email or sends out an instant message, you are the first to respond, what message are you sending? You have basically told everyone that what you're doing is less important than solving their problem. At first, that seems like being a good teammate (and it is!), but over time there's another message you're sending: you will always drop what you're doing to answer a question.

The next time they have a problem, who are they going to go to? They might even stop going to the rest of the team and rely on you. While it feels good to be a resource to your team, this puts an extra strain on getting your own work done.

Here's a paradox central to being a great remote teammate. How can you support your team and be a resource, while at the same time getting your work done and taking care of your own to-do list?

If you have the time, and you can help, do it. That said, here are some simple things you can do that (over time) will help you develop a helpful, equitable relationship with your teammates and help everyone get their work done:

- *Clarify expectations with others.* If you aren't clear about how quickly you must respond or feel you have no control over your time choices, you aren't alone. Many teams don't have explicit conversations about what is a reasonable response time to an email request (usually end of day or within twenty-four hours) or an instant message (usually faster, because it says INSTANT in the name), and so everyone is left to make their own assumptions about what's "reasonable" or "fast."

  Have honest conversations with your peers about response time and how interruptions affect everyone's work. If you can come to an agreement about expectations, including many of the previous suggestions, you are less likely to insult someone or damage an existing relationship while at the same time giving yourself permission to make good time-management choices.

- *Read the request carefully.* Not every question or request requires an immediate response. Is there a stated time frame for a response? If Charlie doesn't need an answer until the end of the day, there's no need to stop what you're doing and answer him right then. You can help your peers by letting them know when you need answers to a problem or a time to talk. Simple directions like "no rush" or "by Friday" will help lower everyone's blood pressure and make your request far clearer. Don't panic if you don't need to. If you don't know when they need it, ask in a way that provides clarity, not a way that raises their defensiveness.

- *Respond with an explanation.* If the issue sounds urgent, or you know you can help, just not right now, don't be afraid to defer the answer with a brief explanation: "I am in the middle of something but can get it to you tomorrow morning; will that work?" Usually the person will understand and wait for you (in which case you're still helping) or go find help elsewhere (so they aren't waiting for something that isn't coming). Silence is far more damaging to relationships than honesty. Remember—assuming serves no one.

- *Use your status updates to set expectations.* How carefully do you manage your online availability? If your Microsoft Teams status says "online" or "available," why is it surprising that people message you? After all, you're online and available. If they think you are there and you don't respond, they have reason to get cranky. If you are engaged in something and can't be interrupted, it makes sense to let people know that. Set your status so people know your true availability. When you do this, remember to change it back when you are available. This applies to shared calendars and time allocated in your project management software as well.

  For example, in Slack you can share your current status. (Most tools have a similar availability feature.) You can also write additional information into your status such as "Working on a project until noon" or "Out of the office but available by phone." This helps set reasonable expectations about response time, and people aren't drumming their fingers waiting for an answer that isn't coming. Your email, collaboration, and instant message tools can be used to protect your time when needed and show availability when you have the bandwidth.

  Another way to do this is to set expectations about response time in the subject line of the email. For example, at The Kevin Eikenberry Group we often write the subject of the email and then "No Rush" or "Need by tomorrow" in the subject line. If there's no need to cause a panic, we try not to create it.

- *Share your calendar, then actively manage it.* If your team doesn't share calendars, why not? This is a simple way to set expectations for everyone, and still respect your time. But simply letting people look at your calendar isn't enough. Most of us put meetings or client time on our calendar, but if you don't schedule time for getting to and from the meeting, project work, or working on something without interruption, all your teammates see is that you're available.

- *Respect the time you block out.* Remember that we've been talking about how we teach people to work with us. If your status says you're unavailable, or you have time blacked out but respond to the email right away, what message are you sending? You are still letting people know their time is more important than yours. Sometimes that's true, but not always. If you respond during time you're scheduled, try an explanation: "We are on a break from class so I can answer you . . ." so people know your time is still being managed.

What Habits Help or Hinder Your Productivity?

The American general and former secretary of state Colin Powell said, "If you are going to achieve excellence in big things, you develop the habit in little matters."

That's a roundabout way of saying that our daily productivity is impacted in all kinds of ways by our habits. Some of those habits—say, turning off the TV when you're working—make you more productive. Others, like leaving Facebook open on your browser when you're working, might add to the distractions.

We are creatures of habit, and what is a boon to one person (maybe you work well with music blasting) may be a barrier to someone else. We won't get into specific habits here, but we do need to take a look at how we reinforce those habits and behaviors that help us get work done and eliminate those that get in the way.

There are some proven approaches to break or change a habit. If you have identified something you know gets in the way of your productivity, here are some ways to alter it:

- *Replace one behavior with another.* This can be as easy as remembering to close your home office door when you start work so you don't get sucked into family drama. Maybe get in the habit of cleaning out the coffee pot before you sit at the keyboard so your brain doesn't become obsessed with the dirty pot when you need to focus on your work. Creating rituals and repeating behavior helps change our habits over time. We'll discuss more of this in chapter 6.

- *Set reminders and make notes to yourself.* Since you know you need to take breaks and eat properly, build those activities into your day. Don't rely on your brain or your stomach. Set timers for breaks, and block lunch on your calendar.

- *Reward your successful change.* Changing some behaviors is incredibly difficult, and there can be short-term pain or discomfort associated with it. If you've ever suffered caffeine or nicotine withdrawal, you know what we're talking about. People change habits when they avoid pain or receive pleasure from the change in what they do. Reward yourself in little ways for doing things right. Engage the pleasure centers of your brain. This can be as simple as allowing yourself to knock off ten minutes early on days when you achieve your goals or having something especially yummy for lunch. Just tie these little rewards to the successfully changed behavior.

- *Start small.* If you try to make huge habit changes, you are far more likely to fail and be demotivated. Let's say your goal is to check email less often. Start by turning off the "ding" notification and only checking your email every thirty minutes. Then you can extend it to sixty. If you start by saying "I'm only going to check my email in the morning and at noon," there's a good chance you might feel like your head will explode, and you won't be able to focus on anything else. Baby steps are still progress.

- *Be patient.* Change is not easy, and habits become habits because we get to the point where we don't think about them, we just do them. Your brain will try to keep doing things the way you've always done them. Some days you'll win, some days your old brain will claim victory. When you engage in the old, negative behavior, just start over. Think of those signs on construction sites that show the number of accident-free days. Replace "accident free" with "ate a healthy breakfast" and carry on.

- *Find support and accountability.* Think about changing big habits such as excessive drinking. One of the basic tenets of organizations like Alcoholics Anonymous is that it is nearly impossible to change by yourself. That's why you must publicly state your goals and have a sponsor (someone you are accountable to and can go to for help). Staying off email while you're supposed to be in a meeting might not be as big a problem, but the concept is the same. Tell a trusted teammate about the change in behavior you're trying to achieve, and ask them to help you be accountable.

Wayne once tried to stop answering emails in the middle of the night, with little success. Finally, he and a friend agreed to hold each other accountable and playfully bust each other's chops when emails had a 2:00 a.m. time stamp. Together they stopped that foolishness.

In the same vein, we suggest you consider telling your manager what you're trying to achieve. One of the highest forms of accountability is to include support in your coaching discussions. When the boss asks, "How are you doing with _____?" the behavior takes on new significance.

- *Learn more about changing your habits.* There are some great resources to help you further. We recommend *Atomic Habits* by James Clear.

Being a productive teammate is more than simply checking the tasks off your list, or "buckling down and working harder." It comes from knowing what needs to be done when, finding ways to get around both systemic and self-created roadblocks, and changing your behavior while supporting the goals of the team.

When you are doubting yourself, or you feel like you don't know which end is up anymore, ask yourself the four pivot questions from the beginning of the chapter. We'll bet you can find the answer and take action.

Pause and Reflect

▶ On most days are you getting enough of the right things done? If not, what is your biggest barrier?

▶ What is your best strategy for "snapping out of it" when you are stuck or unproductive?

Online Resource

For a tool to help you identify habits that block your progress, as well as those you want to further develop, register at the website:

LongDistanceTeammate.com/resources

and request the **Habit Tool**.

Chapter 5

The Power of Establishing Routines

Araceli is new to working from home. At first it was great; she could work in whatever clothes she wanted (and some days those pajamas stayed on until almost noon). She could take time in the middle of the workday to take her kids to school as long as she was reachable by phone, and she wasn't stuck with a commute that ate into personal and family time. But lately, she's noticed that it seems harder than ever to keep work to "work hours." There doesn't seem to be any structure to her day, and what once felt freeing now simply means there's no start or stop to her day. Being always connected is exhausting her, and she's enjoying her work less and less. She wonders why she used to feel more energized than she does now.

When you hear the word *routine*, it conjures up a negative picture that looks like "the same old, same old," or each day being exactly like every other with nothing new to excite or interest us. But the Cambridge Dictionary defines it as "a usual set of activities or way of doing things."[1] No judgment there, just a neutral term—and the point of this chapter.

Other definitions of routine include words like "habit" and "pattern of behavior." That brings us to an important point. While a routine can become boring and uninspiring, developing certain habits and duplicating a successful process can have very real benefits.

Routines can impact any part of our day. We find that the morning or start-of-day routines have the biggest impact on your success or failure as a remote worker.

According to Tracy Kennedy, the personal development expert at Life-hack.org, some of the benefits of establishing a morning (and, as you'll see, an end-of-day) routine include:

- Increasing productivity

- Reducing stress

- Starting the day on the right foot

- Controlling the day, so the day doesn't control you

- Balancing your personal and work life better

Routines Help Increase Productivity

You (and Araceli in our example) might need to be reminded: productivity is not how long you work, or how many hours you put in. Remember that productivity is really the measure of how much valuable work gets done in the time you're being paid to work. Unless you are being paid, or billing, hourly, your focus should be on getting as much done as possible while you are working. Then you can get on with the rest of your life. Remember—make your goal accomplishment, not activity. In fact, feeling like you're working from the moment you get up to long past dinner is one of the leading causes of burnout and ultimately becoming disengaged from your work.

When you work in the office, the day has a rhythm and structure. The real work begins when you get to your desk or job site and ends (more or less—even though emails are always lurking) when you leave for the day. Even if you take work home, the location was a real differentiator that likely doesn't exist anymore. But what happens when your day begins the moment you wake up and your feet touch the floor, and there's no time to ease into your day?

Routines Help Reduce Stress

Since there aren't routines that are automatic due to a commute to the office, questions with obvious answers before now require renewed thought. Consider these examples:

- What time do I really need to get out of bed in the morning?

- What should I eat for breakfast?

- How will I have time to exercise or play with the dog?

- What will I wear?

- Which of the many tasks I face today will I tackle first?

If you break your day into component pieces, you probably make a hundred decisions before lunch, and many of those will impact your productivity. While deciding what to wear probably isn't the most agonizing choice you'll have to make, it requires energy and brain cells that could be used better somewhere else.

Have you ever started returning phone calls while the coffee is brewing, and find that it's ten o'clock and you still haven't had breakfast? If so, you've been hungry and grumpy—and probably gotten less done than you could have.

One advantage of establishing a healthy, mindful morning routine is that you can reduce some of the stressors in your life and train yourself literally not to think of them until it's time.

Routines Help You Start the Day on the Right Foot

Remember when we said that time management is choice management? That mindset begins with how you choose to structure your day. Yes, you might have to respond to that irate customer when the day starts, but there's no reason to let that ruin your morning. If you've had your coffee, gone for a walk, had breakfast with your family, and maybe meditated or prayed or however you get yourself centered, when your workday actually begins you'll be more mentally prepared to tackle whatever awaits you.

In many cases, you get to decide (or at least negotiate) when your workday begins and ends. You can actively choose to do positive, grounding activities that prepare you for the day. Time zones and the demands of your job might not let you live an old-fashioned, precise, nine-to-five existence, but if you wanted that you probably wouldn't be working from home anyway—and remember you don't have to commute either! By being prepared and mentally grounded, you will be ready to tackle the challenges of your job and do them more effectively.

Routines Help You Control Your Day Rather Than Let It Control You

You might feel out of control when you start your day by checking your phone then leaping into action while—still in your pajamas. That's a pretty rocky start when you haven't had your first cup of coffee, had a chance to get a hug from your little ones, or looked out the window and seen the sunrise.

Do you look at your phone in the morning with one eye open, afraid to see what's awaiting you? Even if you started by looking at the phone when you worked in the office, you had to stop and get ready to leave for work. Now you aren't "leaving" to go anywhere. When you leave your desk at the end of the day, do you still stare at your phone, answering email during dinner?

Use the start and end of your day to create structure that allows you to begin and end your work and then engage in the other parts of your life that matter.

How to Build a Healthy, Productive Morning Routine

Maybe you are a morning person, or perhaps you hit the snooze button five times and still resent getting up. Some people drink coffee; others can't stand it. Not enough of us exercise, but those who do need to find the time. There is no such thing as a standard, one-size-fits-all way to face the day. There are some best practices and rules of thumb to establish habits to start your day as a remote worker:

- Give yourself time to breathe and open your eyes before reaching for your phone.

- Be mindful of answering messages before you start work. If you absolutely must respond to an email or a message at the start of the day, make sure it's only that one, and return to your morning.

- Set a schedule or routine. If you're going to exercise or walk the dog, do it at the same time every day. If you keep thinking about doing it, but don't know when you'll find the time, the thought of it will be a stress inducer and will offset the pleasure of the walk itself.

- Eat a healthy breakfast. Some people (like Wayne) need to eat as soon as they get up—and like a big breakfast. Other people can go a while before eating or can make do with very little. You know the foods that energize you (proteins, healthy grains, fruit) and those that drain your energy (sugars and processed foods). The important thing is that you build your dietary habits into your routine or you'll find yourself grabbing whatever is handy, or fastest, and it's seldom the best for you.

- End your day as mindfully as you begin it. The end-of-the-day ritual can be as important as the beginning. Without something that tells your brain, "okay, we're at work now," you'll start work before you're mentally prepared. Similarly, if you don't do something to signify you're off duty, your brain will nag at you to keep working. Turn off the lights in your home office. Close your laptop entirely.

Since you don't have a commute or office hours to create these rituals for you, you need to do it yourself.

What do we mean by ritual? Here's a simple example.

Wayne has worked from home for the last twelve years or so—but he remembers how difficult it was for him at first. It turns out he needs more structure than he'd like to admit. But over time, he's created a system that works for him. Your mileage may vary.

First, Wayne lives in the Pacific time zone while most of his teammates in The Kevin Eikenberry Group are on East Coast (US) time. That means when Wayne rolls out of bed about six a.m., the workday has already started for most people.

The first decision is whether or not to check his messages. Because he's a good teammate, he'll check his email and instant messages to see if anything is impacting the work of others already this morning. He'll also discover whether or not his to-do list requires adjusting. If he must respond to a message, he will. Otherwise he puts his phone down and begins his day.

The coffee goes on and he watches the local news, weather, and sports scores. He grabs breakfast while finding out how his hockey team did (which may or may not help his digestion).

Then he showers, gets dressed in work-appropriate clothes, and makes the bed. Experience (and considerable research) shows that most people become more work oriented and focused if there is a standard behavior that separates the workday from the rest of their lives.

When Wayne goes into the office (usually around seven o'clock), he turns on his laptop, changes his status on email and Slack to "active," and begins the day. He is dressed for work, has had time to be mindful about what the day will look like, and is physically and mentally ready to take on the world.

At the end of the day, he checks his email one last time, adjusts the status on his email and Slack to "away," and heads downstairs. Yes, he has his phone with him, and if it's important he will take a phone call or answer a message, but he's not expected to be on call at all hours, and he's getting better about responding only to those things that are truly urgent.

By establishing a routine that allows him to be focused, to be healthy, and to have a firm but flexible start and end to the day, he's able to feel okay about turning work off.

What are the things you need to get a good start on your day? Are you allowing yourself to do them? How can you build exercise, healthy diet, and work-life balance into your life?

All of it starts with creating a routine to start and end your day.

Pause and Reflect

► What morning routines serve you well?

► Which do you need to create or change?

► If you work in a vastly different time zone from your teammates, how aware are you of each other's preferred start and end times?

Part 2

Skills to Help You Succeed

Hector has been working on projects for as long as he can remember. He was confident in his work and generally received good feedback over the years. When he found out he would be working from home, he was excited. He lost his commute, and since the work was the same, his confidence was as strong as his outlook. Now that he has been working from home for a few months, he isn't quite so sure. It is still project work, but more seems different than he expected. Doing work the way he always did isn't always getting him the same results he got before—and it shows in the feedback he is receiving. He wants to succeed, but now he realizes he needs to change or polish his skills—but doesn't know where to start.

Because we don't know the specific nature of your work, we can't help you with the technical parts of your job. This part outlines the skills that take you far beyond technical expertise. In fact, these are the skills that will allow you to work successfully with others—especially in a remote or virtual setting. Being able to build trust, communicate more effectively, set clear expectations, and more will keep you from tearing your hair out—these skills have personal benefits for your sanity. But we hope as you read these chapters you set a higher bar for yourself than that.

This book is about helping you engage and connect in new and more profound ways with your work and your teammates. To do that requires you to build and hone a new set of skills. When you look at the titles of the chapters in this part, you may be tempted to say, "I already know that."

Maybe you do.

But if you are like Hector, or you know that working remotely is taxing your skills and pushing you to the limit of your ability to succeed, read on and read carefully. Each of these skills matters wherever you work, but we're giving you specific examples and approaches for doing all these things when working at a distance.

Chapter 6

Getting Clear
Expectations for Your Work

Lin is frustrated and hurt. She has been working on this project for several months and felt like she was doing well. She met her deadlines, and no one has been critical or told her she was missing anything. In fact, she was hoping to get the lead on the follow-up project and had never even considered not at least having her contract extended for that one. Today she's learned differently—apparently, among other things, her communication with other team members wasn't what was needed. When this project is over, she'll be looking for a new project with a different organization.

While blind to it, Lin is experiencing a gap between what was expected of her and what she was delivering. While she thought she was doing fine, meeting her expectations and doing her job at every turn, apparently that wasn't the case. While it might seem obvious, when we don't know what is expected of us, it is nearly impossible to succeed. Unfortunately, unclear expectations are the rule more than the exception, especially for remote workers.

This gets directly at "Productivity" from our model: Without clear expectations, how can you even measure your productivity in a meaningful way?

What Is Expected?

Okay, so having clear expectations of the work is important; but you might think, "If I work hard and pay attention, won't I be successful?"

Maybe, and only if you are lucky.

Clear job expectations are more than what is written in the job description. With all due respect to our friends in human resources departments, the purpose of a job description is to give us a picture of the landscape, to offer a high-level picture of the work. But if you stay at that high level, you will miss the details, specific benchmarks, and unwritten and unspoken rules of your team that truly define success in your work.

You want your expectations to be completely clear (think Jack Nicholson in the movie *A Few Good Men*—"crystal clear") and not just clear to you but mutually understood. It's not enough to be clear, until you know that your understanding matches others'.

If you have that with your leader, great; you are in a much better place. But if you have ever had a moment like Lin's in our opening story, or ever wonder if you are doing what your leader wants, we are going to help you solve that dilemma and reduce any anxiety it might cause.

Why Does It Matter?

While being clear on what success looks like should be reason enough for having precise expectations of your work, there are other reasons that matter too—and each one is even more important when you don't bump into people in the hallway every day. The other benefits of clear expectations include:

- *Greater confidence.* When you know what needs to be done, by when, and how well, you will immediately have greater confidence. Even if you aren't sure how to achieve all that, knowing it sets the path for greater confidence. And greater confidence leads to . . .

- *Greater results.* Bottom line—when you know what is expected, your odds of achieving it go up. Knowing the mark you are aiming at is half the battle. Lin didn't achieve success in part because she apparently wasn't aiming at the right target.

- *Greater trust.* We'll say much more about trust in chapter 10, but think about it this way. If I know what you expect of me, I have a better chance of delivering. And if I deliver, trust between us builds. One of the best ways to ensure that trust is growing is by having mutually clear expectations.

- *Less conflict.* One of the biggest sources of workplace conflict is unclear expectations between two people or groups. When everyone thinks "someone else was supposed to do it," or "everyone knows how it's done here," but the work *doesn't* get done—expectations weren't clear. The risk of this is higher, and the problems caused by it are worse, when people don't work closely together. Hint—this isn't just with your leader. We'll say more about that in a minute.

Whose Expectations Matter?

The expectations that your leader has of you and your teammates, as the representatives of those who write your paycheck, matter for sure. But those aren't the only expectations that you need to be aware of and work to understand and meet. Even though you work *remotely,* you don't work *alone.* Consider the following:

- *Your teammates.* You finish your work product so Bonnie in IT can use it. Do you know what she uses it for, what matters to her, and how you might make her life easier?

- *Members of a project team.* There was a kickoff meeting and weekly updates, but how clear are you on what is expected of you on all those project tasks? How will people communicate with you—and in what format? This should be a normal part of the project process, but we've all experienced surprises when we thought everyone was on the same page and they weren't.

- *Customers.* If you interact directly with the paying customer, do you know what their expectations are?

Those broad categories capture most everyone whose expectations you might need to consider—if you think of a person or group that applies in your case, add them to your personal list. We have left one person off, though.

You.

While we've convinced you that understanding the expectations of others will serve everyone, we didn't mention you.

In any of these working relationships, including with your leader, you have expectations too. Working in ways that meet the expectations of others is critical to your success, but those efforts need to go both ways. Don't be a wallflower or a pushover—but don't be a demanding bully either. Remember that there is a difference between declaring "This is what I expect!" and creating a conversation where everyone can be clearer about how you will work together. As you create a clear understanding of what is expected of you, share your expectations of the other people as well.

What resources do you need to succeed? What don't you understand about the project or process? Make sure you know how the customer or your teammate uses your work output, so you can deliver it even more effectively for them.

What Should Be Included in "Clear Expectations"?

So far, we have mostly been talking about expectations in a general way. But what are the specific things that might be included? When you have clarity from your leader (or the others we just talked about) in each of these areas, you can be sure that you are both on the same page. Let's start with the most obvious:

- *The work itself.* Do you know what is required of you on that report you must write? Do you know how others will judge if you did something well? Teachers in school use rubrics to define for students what is expected and how they will be graded. Having that rubric helps students know what is required. Your report card might not have A's and B's on it, but you get report cards at work through performance reviews and feedback. Knowing what is expected in relationship to the work itself improves your chances of success!

- *The quality of the work.* The rubric usually goes beyond simply completing the work to the quality of the work. Make sure you know more than that you are supposed to write the report; make sure you know what needs to be included, what the right level of detail is, and who your audience is. You've had work delivered to you that wasn't of the quality or completeness you needed. How did that feel to you? When you are clear on the quality expectations, you will more likely deliver what others need.

- *Why the work is being done.* This is often left out, because the other party, knowing the situation well, assumes everyone knows why this work is being done. This assumption is often the biggest cause of expectation gaps. When you have the big picture and a clear context of why, many of the other expectations that follow make perfect sense. When you don't have that picture, you make your own assumptions based on how you see the world or how you did things at your last job. Remember this: assumptions are the enemy of clear expectations, and never serve anyone.

- *The timeliness of the work.* We bet that you care about when you get work or input from others. Perhaps your biggest frustration is waiting for people to get things to you. How are you supposed to get your job done if you don't have everything you need? Do you suppose others care about that from you too? Do you know when people need things from you? This is a leading cause of tension when thinking about the "your work" and "team work" boxes (refer to figure 2 in chapter 2).

- *Communication about the work.* Here are just a few of the questions you need answers to: How much communication does your boss need from you as you work? Do you know what they need from you in terms of updates, how willing they are to get questions from you? Do they want your questions as stream of consciousness, as you think of them, or sent once a day/week/month? What communication media do they prefer or require? This isn't a complete list but gives you a good start. We'll discuss this more in the next chapter.

- *How the work is done.* Communication is in this bucket, but it is a bigger bucket (more like a barrel, perhaps), and along with the "why," this area is often murky. We are talking about the culture of the organization. How are you to operate to be successful? What approaches and strategies will help you get along and get ahead? Since culture is the unspoken "how we do things around here," and since you are working remotely and not in the middle of things where we often pick information up without noticing, it might take a long time to figure this out. Equally frustrating, while you are trying to figure it out, you might be missing the expectations others have for you. If you are remote and joined the organization that way (as opposed to moving home after working on-site), this may be the biggest area of opportunity for you to gain clarity.

How to Make Expectations Clear

You may be thinking, this is all fine, guys, but I need to give this chapter to my boss—*they* are the ones who need to do this stuff. They are in charge, and it is their responsibility to give me clear expectations.

Yes, it is their responsibility. But if your expectations aren't clear, you have two choices. Wait for them (and whine because "they aren't doing their job") or step up and ask questions and initiate the conversation yourself.

I bet you know which choice we recommend—remember "Proactivity" from the 3P Model?

Kevin often says, "Reading your manager's mind isn't in your job description." We could say the same in reverse. Don't expect your leader to be able to read yours either. Don't automatically assume the worst—they have plenty on their plate. Your manager likely doesn't realize the expectations aren't clear to you. They may believe they told you (and even if they did, once, eleven months ago, that doesn't mean they were clear then or now).

Is it possible they are bungling their job and are inept? Yes. Is it also possible that they just don't know you aren't clear? Yes. As you sit here now, unclear, does the reason matter? Not at all.

Remember that the responsibility for having clear expectations rests with both parties—whether between you and your leader, your teammates, or customers. If you aren't clear, you can—and should—do something about it.

Thinking about having this conversation with your leader might seem hard. You may be wondering how to go about it, and you might be worried about coming across as harsh or difficult. We believe that you can be kind and clear. Author Brené Brown turns that thought around and writes:

> **Over the past several years, my team and I have learned something about clarity and the importance of hard conversations that has changed everything from the way we talk to each other to the way we negotiate with external partners. It's simple but transformative: Clear is kind. Unclear is unkind.[1]**

If you are ready to be clearer, and be kind as you do it, here are a series of steps you can take to create clearer expectations for yourself (and the other person too):

1. *Ask for time to have this conversation.* This will likely take some time, so schedule specific time for this important work. Let them know what you want to accomplish and why. This will allow them to come prepared too.

2. *Create a series of questions.* These bullet points are a start, or you can use the checklist you can download from the instructions at the end of the chapter. Depending on your specific situation and relationship with your boss, you might consider sharing these questions before the meeting. If you do, make sure they understand your asking comes from a place of curiosity, not demand.

3. *Be clear on what you need.* Yes, you are trying to understand their expectations, but since this will be a conversation, knowing what your needs are makes sense too. If you can't explain them to yourself, it might not make sense to the other person.

4. *Have an open conversation.* Since the expectations must be mutually clear, keep the conversation open and moving toward that goal.

5. *Write the expectations and metrics down.* We aren't talking about a legal document here, but when things are written down, we can both remember them! If you want clearly defined, mutually understood expectations, put them in writing.

6. *Agree and commit.* After all, this is why you started this process.

Final Thoughts

Getting clear expectations is work worth doing, but perhaps unfortunately, it isn't a one-and-done activity. You know that circumstances change, and when things change, expectations need to be discussed, revised, or reconfirmed.

Here's one simple example. Wayne and his bride were tired of the cold winters in Chicago and decided to move to Las Vegas. Since Kevin (and the bulk of the team) live in the Eastern time zone, some things changed for all of us as Wayne unpacked his bags. While not every expectation between Kevin and Wayne (and Wayne and other teammates) changed with the time zone, some did (like what time Wayne is available for meetings), and we needed to discuss and recalibrate.

That is a simple one, but here is the rule of thumb—if something changes, recheck expectations. Some of those changes include:

- A new leader

- New teammates

- New senior leadership

- New products

- New processes

- New projects

- New communication tools

- New laws or regulations

One more: the passage of time. As we stated earlier, assuming serves no one. To be an engaged and connected remote teammate means that you take responsibility for continuing to make sure you are delivering what others need.

Being blissfully unaware of what others want and need from you as you work in your home office or at your kitchen table isn't blissful for long. The fact that you interact with others less frequently and rarely even face-to-face makes this harder and more important. But when you get it right you will get better results for everyone. Your efforts to create clarity will be noticed—because everyone benefits, and your proactivity created those benefits.

Pause and Reflect

▶ What frustrates you about working with others now? Are these frustrations caused by a gap in expectations?

▶ If you share clear expectations with someone—how did that happen?

▶ What can you learn from that experience to create clearer ones with others?

Online Resource

For a checklist to help you begin an expectation conversation with your boss or teammates, register at the website:

LongDistanceTeammate.com/resources

and request the **Expectation Conversations**.

Chapter 7

Creating Great Remote Communication

Sandra is more introverted than most and thought working from home would be a joyful experience. Communication would be about business matters and nothing more. She thought she'd be able to focus more completely on her work and worry less about having to constantly interact with others. Sam is far more extroverted than Sandra and was worried about working remotely. He was afraid he would miss the energy and interaction that comes from being around people. While Sandra and Sam are both partially right, the communication skills needed when working remotely aren't related simply to the amount of communication.

Both Sandra and Sam (and you) need to navigate the use of tools that mediate the communication; both need to understand that how they communicate is even more important than it was when they worked in the office.

When thinking about remote communication, many people start with the fact that there will be less of it. And while there may be less "How was your weekend?" or "Did you see that score in the game last night?" that's only the beginning of the challenges you'll face. In this chapter we will talk about more than the amount of communication, but also the quality and approaches required. Specifically, you will leave with skills that will help you communicate better in any remote working situation now and in the future.

Why Should You Worry about This?

Why should we even worry about remote communication? The obvious answer is that communication is inherently harder at a distance. It is hard enough across the desk from each other—and everything that distance adds makes it more challenging. In any organization either of us have ever consulted with or interacted with, people have said that communication could be better. Since it is harder remotely, we are going to give you a variety of ideas and share some skills, but let's talk about the importance of effective, intentional communication to organizational life and success.

- *Great communication = great results.* You can't get the kind of results you want and need—whether on daily work output, on projects large or small, or in the big organizational picture—without solid communication. If you don't have it, you need it.

- *It is the "stuff" of work.* You might forget that when you're working by yourself in your own little world at home and no one else is around. And yet everything that happens at work requires communication, inside or outside the organization. That's why we say that communication is the stuff of work.

- *Poor communication creates rework.* If you are honest with yourself, there have been times this week when you've seen rework happening. If you look at the cause of doing something over, and doing it again, you will almost always find that the message was poorly constructed, or misinterpreted, or ignored, if it was sent at all.

- *Poor communication causes stress.* If we take only that rework situation (but we could all cite more examples), the stress caused by the rework itself, the frustration, and other negative emotions all come from the poor communication. Want less stress in your work? Become a better communicator.

- *Poor communication causes conflict.* If our messages were always crystal clear, if people understood (and lived up to) the expectations of others, the amount of conflict you experience would be drastically reduced.

- *Poor communication reduces productivity.* Put all these points together and the endpoint is clear: all communication gaps reduce productivity.

It is possible as you read this list, you are thinking about other people, thinking that if you could get those people (insert the names of your choice) to communicate better, you would have better results.

Stop. Right. There.

Everyone is responsible for communication success.

This isn't the chapter for you to give to someone else to read or for you to skim while you think about them. If you want better communication in your work situation, you must recognize that *creating better remote communication starts with you.*

As you read this chapter, you will gain ideas for improving your communication success. It is up to you to think of who in your life and work it will apply to most. Perhaps it is your leader, your teammates, a specific teammate, the leader of that special project you are on, people in other departments, or even customers. As you read, decide on the specific people or groups where making some changes could help you be a better communicator.

The Core of Communication

If you've ever taken a class on communication in your life, in high school, in college, or on the job, chances are in the first chapter of the textbook and in the first lecture, there was a conversation about communication as something that takes place between people. There was likely even an image with some arrows pointing to senders and receivers.

Let's simplify that. Communication is message sent, message received, and message understood.

Simple, right?

- *Message sent.* You must know what you want to send, and then send it through some media (your voice, email, passenger pigeon, or whatever).

- *Message received.* The message you sent must be heard, received, and accepted by the other person. If it isn't, you were just talking or typing.

- *Message understood.* Reception isn't enough either. Until the receiver interprets and understands your message, you don't have true communication.

Most of us focus on the first part. You've said or thought things like this a hundred times: "How many times do I have to tell them?" "I sent them the email," "I told them yesterday," "What part of no don't they understand?" These comments or thoughts are all about message sent, ignoring the other two parts of true communication.

It is natural to focus on message sent, because that is the only part of the process you can directly control. You can control the content as well as when and how you convey your message. Working remotely, you decide whether to email, send a chat or instant message, pick up the phone, fire up the webcam, or whatever. You control sending.

You *do not* have control over others receiving or correctly understanding what you sent. But while you can't control "message received" and "message understood," you can influence those things. The best communicators recognize that they need to always be thinking about how they can *improve the chances* of the audience correctly receiving and understanding the message. That is the fundamental question for communicators, and when you're working remotely, it is harder still because you can't stop by their office and have a conversation. The face-to-face, one-on-one conversation gives you the best odds for getting your messages received and understood.

When working remotely, that's not an option—which means we must get better at communication, because it is more important and harder than ever.

How Our Message Is Received

If you want to communicate more clearly, you must understand how human beings receive messages. Simply put, our intended audience receives messages from us in three ways:

- *What we say.* Here we are talking about the words we actually say or use. Usually this is the verbal part of communication—specifically, the verbiage that we use. It is the transcript of the conversation, the actual words, and the content of the message itself. That is how we are communicating with you right now, with our words. This, of course, includes the words of any written communication you send.

- *How we say it.* This is the vocal component. It's the audio recording, where others can hear tone, pitch, pace, and volume. It is intonation and emphasis. It's what you emphasize and how you emphasize it using your voice. Tone also shows up in writing. Have you ever read an IM and thought, "She sounds angry"? IMs don't make noise, but you got a feeling (right or wrong) about their mood and intentions nonetheless.

- *How we look.* This is the visual part. Part of the message is carried through the sender's eye contact, facial expressions, and gestures. It's everything else. If *what we say* is the transcript, and *how we say it* is the audio recording, *how we look* is the video. While we can't see the sender in an email, if it is full of typos, or is badly formatted, this may "look" wrong and people will draw conclusions about the sender (and to our point here, the message). This may interfere with your message being understood or accepted the way you wish.

Each of these plays a role. And while we as senders like to place a heavy focus on our word choices, when you stop and think about it (especially when you think about it as a receiver), you realize that as important as the words are, they are a relatively small part of how people receive our messages.

Our Communication Tool Options

As we discussed in *The Long-Distance Leader*, the main difference between working in a central location and working remotely is that we rely much more heavily on technology to connect us to our teammates when we're apart. Before we go any further into our communication discussion, we should be clear about the types of tools available.

You'll notice that in most cases we haven't been specific about which tools to use. Rather, we've talked about "instant messaging" or "webcams" instead of "Jabber" or "Zoom." That is for a couple of reasons:

- We think the types of tools matter; the specific brand or platform is less important.

- Technology changes at an alarming rate, and we don't want to date ourselves or alienate you by referring to something that is quickly outdated or replaced.

Kevin and Wayne know this intimately. We began writing this book in early 2020, before the coronavirus changed the way we work. At the time, Zoom was an emerging but still niche tool. By May 2020, a mere three months later, it had become the go-to webcam platform for a lot of people. It got to the point where it became a running joke on *Saturday Night Live* and even became a generic verb. Everyone knows what "I was on a Zoom" or "I was Zooming with Bob" means.

Further proof is that during that time, Google Hangouts changed to Google Meet to further compete with Zoom, and nobody knows how popular or widespread it will be by the time you read this. The point of this book is to talk about the various types of tools, which will remain true for a long time without becoming obsolete when another technology or platform emerges.

What are the types of tools that all good remote and hybrid teams need to have at their disposal? While some tools serve multiple purposes, they break down roughly into the following categories. We are using examples as of the writing of this book to make it as clear as possible:

- *Telephony.* As odd as it seems to many of us, not too long ago this was the main way people communicated when they were apart. Real-time voice conversations still matter when you need to talk things out with team-mates or the whole group. This can include old-fashioned land lines, cell phones, or network tools like RingCentral, Citrix, or other Voice over IP (VoIP) phone systems.

- *Asynchronous written and text-based communication.* Today's dispersed workers do more in writing than at any time in history. As a result, we have many ways to communicate in writing. These tools include shared word processing software like Microsoft Word, Office 365, and Google Docs. It also includes email applications such as Outlook and Gmail. SMS texting is also a form of asynchronous writing.

- *Synchronous unified communication and collaboration.* "All-in-one" solutions that allow for chat, text, file transfer, and other functions in a single platform are the fastest growing segment of team collaboration tools. These tools include Microsoft Teams, Slack, Google Meet, Jabber, and many others. They are most often used for real-time chat, either in groups or one on one. They put the "instant" in instant message.

- *Videoconferencing.* Sometimes videoconferencing consists of stand-alone tools like the original Skype, FaceTime, the basic Zoom package, and Google Meet. Other times these tools can be built into other suites of programs. Microsoft Teams has Skype capabilities built in. Slack easily integrates with Zoom for fast and simple webcam conversations.

- *Web meeting and screen sharing tools.* While all good web-meeting platforms include video chat, not all video chat tools make for great meetings. Good virtual meeting tools include more than video and webcam. They also have whiteboards, recording functions, built-in chat, polling features, and screen sharing with remote control. More robust web-meeting platforms include Webex, GoToMeeting, Adobe Connect, the new Google Meet, and the professional version of Zoom.

- *Project management tools.* Software packages like Basecamp, Microsoft Project, Monday, OneNote, and too many others to count are designed to allow teams to find and share vital information in a hurry. Users can track progress on projects, check the status of action items, ask and answer questions, and create consistent reports.

- *Cloud file sharing services.* Your organization might have an intranet solution that allows everyone to share files, documents, and information with others over the web. Other companies work on a smaller, team-centric basis. Useful tools that allow people to search for, store, and share information across the network include SharePoint, Google Drive, Dropbox, and Evernote.

- *Cloud-based customer relationship management (CRM) and enterprise platforms.* While these are often thought of as operations or sales and marketing tools, Salesforce, SAP, and other tools increasingly integrate other features to allow teammates to do most of their work on a single screen without having a separate log-on for each function.

What's next? Nobody knows what we will be using to connect, build relationships, pass vital information, and get our work done in a year or five years from now. But the specific tool will be far less important than choosing the right type of tool and using it effectively to work together.

The tools we use are critical to communicating effectively. Being mindful of how each tool impacts your success is part of thinking productively and proactively.

When you work at a distance from some or all of your teammates, you lose the face-to-face communication option and must rely on other media to deliver your message. On the surface, they fall into the three areas we just discussed:

- *What we say* tools include email, IMs, and text messages.

- *How we say it* tools include the phone, a voice mail, a teleconference, and perhaps your web platform when you talk in real time.

- *How we look* tools include your web platform and anytime you use your webcam or recorded video.

If you simply stop here and think about what you've just read—that the words alone rarely carry our entire message—you will realize that as remote teammates, you and everyone else are spending too much time using the tools in the first bucket and not enough time including the vocal and the visual in your communications. Email and IM may be fast and easy but don't always convey all the message. Simply acting on that insight will make you a better remote communicator, and likely a more effective remote teammate.

Picking the Right Tool

Since you have a seemingly endless array of technology, that means you can choose the right tool from those options. On Kevin's farm he has at least ten hammers. While he has a favorite, to effectively do the job at hand, he must pick the best hammer (tool) for the job. The implication for you? Just because you love or are comfortable with one tool (email?) doesn't mean it is the best tool in each situation. In fact, it probably isn't.

Our general advice is, using tools that give you more than just the words alone improves your chances of getting your message received. This doesn't mean there isn't a time and place for instant messages and emails (we use them all the time), but it does mean you can be more intentional in choosing how to communicate and, in doing so, get better results.

Here are four questions to ask yourself when you are ready to be more intentional about which communication tool to use. Thinking through these questions and acting on your answers will improve your odds of successful communication:

- *What is the purpose?* What am I trying to accomplish with this communication? Am I trying to engender a conversation? In which case, email is the poorest possible option. Ask yourself, What's the purpose of the communication, and does that give me a key or a clue as to which tool I ought to pick?

- *What is the timing?* Do people need this information right away? What tool gets people's attention fastest? How urgent is it? Email is a great tool—you can send a message now, and others can read it in ten minutes or an hour; and four hours, and six hours, and it's still there. It remains the same. But if you need to have that conversation sooner, then email might not be the best way to handle it.

- *What am I communicating?* In most any normal workday, as remote workers, we will likely use at least four different tools—we will send emails, send instant messages, fire up our webcam, and make phone calls. In every case, we try to think about what we are actually communicating and how that tool will help.

- *Who is my audience?* If you know that people have a preference, then you might bow to that preference a little bit as long as it still makes sense with the other factors we have been talking about. In other words, if it really doesn't matter for the other choices, the other questions of whether you send a text or an email, then maybe you say, Well, where does that person seem to work best? Or what seems to be best for them? If you know this or have had a conversation with them about it (along the lines of what we talked about in chapter 6 about expectations), then consider their preference. This should be the final question, though—don't just go with their preference if it isn't going to support successful communication.

We introduced the Richness versus Scope Model (figure 3) in *The Long-Distance Leader*, which is a model we adapted from the great work of Bettina Büchel.[1]

Using this model as our guide, the richest communication is two people face-to-face. We have all the verbal, vocal, and visual clues, and we therefore have the best chance of getting our message received by the other person. The reality of remote work is we don't have this ideal communication situation very often. Scope, on the other hand, is about the reach of the communication. That one-on-one, face-to-face conversation? Very low scope. An email sent to an entire team? Possibly very high scope—everyone received the message—and the written message was the same—at the same time.

This suggests that in all remote communication you are balancing richness versus scope—and that if you consider that, you will likely make a better tool choice in any situation. We include this model because along with the four questions we recommend asking yourself, it gives you a way to make better choices about how to send your messages so they are more likely received and understood.

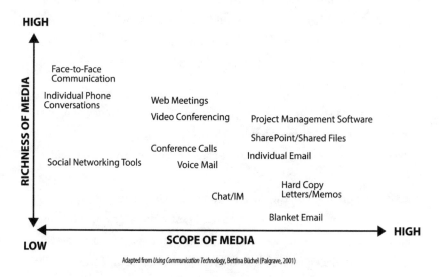

Figure 3. Richness versus Scope Model

More about Email

Email, because it is so used, and misused, when communicating remotely, deserves some words itself. While the points we have already shared likely have you thinking about email differently, there are things you can do to improve how you use email, and how you help your teammates use it too. Here are some specific tips:

- *Tell people what you need.* Too often people ask questions or for more information in an email without making a clear request. Let people know what you need and when you need it. This helps them and gets you what you need with fewer nudges and frustration. For example, "Can you tell me how much we spent on maintenance last year?" is different from "I need to know how much we spent on maintenance last year for the meeting on Thursday."

- *Use the subject line differently.* Sometimes all you need is a question in the subject line. When Kevin sends those, he uses the old editor mark of "<eom>" at the end, which stands for "end of message." If your email contains a question or requires a response, put "[Response Required]" at the front of the subject line, or if the message is information only, consider starting the subject line with "[FYI]." Doing these things helps everyone's productivity but will improve communication success too.

- *Be careful who you include.* Email and text messages can provide great scope, but just because you could copy everyone doesn't mean you have to. Think about who needs to receive the message and add people, rather than start with everyone and then delete from there. Chances are you won't delete many. A simple approach is if the message needs to be read and responded to, put the reader's name in the "to" line. If you are just keeping them in the loop or there's no action required, put them in the "cc" line. This helps people decide which emails get immediate attention.

- *Stop before choosing "reply all."* Do we need to say more about this? If your message is for one or two people, for the sake of everyone's sanity, don't choose "reply all."

- *Don't use it for conversations.* You've been on an email chain that didn't go so well, right? Three or four emails in, the communication gets more confusing, less clear, and the chance for conflict or misunderstanding rises with each keystroke. Our rule at The Kevin Eikenberry Group is three emails in, someone needs to pick up the phone or fire up the webcam, instead of typing and replying. People need to talk because email is not going to cut it. It's probably going to make things worse, not better.

- *Consider using emoticons.* Don't immediately dismiss these as childish or unnecessary. Some emoticons (a smiley face or a thumbs up, for example) can provide richness and context to a message that will otherwise be missing in a text-only communication. Less may be more—and like any communication, consider your audience. An email to the CEO likely requires a different level of formality than an IM or a text to a friend.

Email is a tool you do and should use when working remotely. Tips like these will help you use it for more successful communication.

Beyond Tools

Using the right tools and using them well are just part of the story. Here are some other ideas that will help you communicate remotely. Applying any one of these will repay your investment in this book many times over.

Think Audience First

You know your message, but getting it received requires that you think about your audience. Perhaps you are familiar with one of the many communication/behavioral style models (we are proponents of DISC). If you are, think about the style of those you interact with regularly and determine how you can flex your style to improve the odds of successful results. If you aren't familiar, we suggest you consider using one of these tools to help you become a better communicator. So, remember, it's more than just about the tactical sending of the message.

It's more than work style or personal preference, though—think about what your audience (whether one or many) already knows, cares about, and finds important. Speaking or communicating with them from their perspective will keep you from going into too much depth, or not providing enough context either. Again, make it about the receiver and how you can tailor it for them.

Focus on "Message Received"

As a sender, focus more on getting your message received. Since you are communicating using tools that reduce the richness of communication, make sure you check for understanding and create feedback loops.

If someone is across the table from you, you may naturally ask "Does that make sense?" "What is missing?" or "What isn't clear?" Questions like these create a chance to find out if they understand. Unfortunately, you don't have the same nonverbal information coming back to you if you're communicating asynchronously—in email, for example.

You can create a feedback loop in asynchronous communications by including things like:

- Questions? Let me know.

- If this doesn't make sense, let me know.

- Let me know what concerns you might have, and here's how to share them.

When creating your feedback loop, be as specific as needed: "Drop me an email or get back to me by end of day Thursday."

When you check for understanding, you are confirming receipt of your message—either they got it, or they didn't. More than improving the reception of the message, it creates the chance for a two-way conversation (even if that conversation needs to move to another medium).

When you are the receiver of the message, you can create and close a feedback loop too. We are big believers in the phrase "got it" in IMs and texts and even in emails. We bet that you have sent an IM, a text, or an email to someone and you didn't really know if they were going to take action on it because you never got anything back. Does that give you great confidence in the situation, the person, or the communication?

In a text or your instant message tool, you can use a thumbs up emoticon to do the same thing—it confirms that the instant message was received.

Since communication involves both parties, you can take responsibility from either side. As a sender, ask questions and encourage feedback. As the receiver, you can really help the sender by closing the communication loop with some sort of confirmation that they were heard and understood.

Listen More Carefully

As a receiver, be more careful about your listening and remember that you listen with more than just your ears. If communication were just "what we say," then your ears, your listening, would be like playing back a tape—but you know there's more to it than that. When you work harder at being a better listener, being a better receiver, you'll improve the chances of receiving the message correctly. Active listening is hard enough when face-to-face. To be an effective remote teammate (and communicator), you must work even harder to demonstrate that you are receiving and understanding the message. And guess what? Next time the other person will more likely listen to you too.

You improve the chances that your messages are received when you do a better job of listening, creating feedback loops, and making sure that people get the full message. Here's the thing. When you're using the text-only tools, it's hard to know if people receive and understand your message: that they're "listening." That's why we believe you ought to be picking up the phone and turning on your webcam more frequently.

If the communication is text based, the equivalent of listening is reading for understanding. If you are like us, sometimes you skim emails instead of reading them closely for understanding. When we don't read closely, we create more than miscommunication. After all, how did you feel the last time someone asked you a question that you answered by cutting and pasting from the email you already sent?

It's More Than the Message

How and how effectively we communicate impacts more than "message received." In chapter 9 we will talk about your relationships as a remote teammate. Without question, your effectiveness as a communicator impacts your relationships. More directly, the better you are as a communicator, the better your working relationships will be.

Be More Intentional

Lastly, be more intentional about your communication: the what, when, why, and how all matter. Being intentional ties directly into the "Proactivity" part of the 3P Model. This is the best way to end this chapter, because it is the big idea from it: we urge you to be thinking about the tools, approaches, and audience, not just the message itself. When you make these choices intentionally, rather than from preference or routine, you will get better communication outcomes.

Pause and Reflect

▶ How often do you use the best available tool for your communication goal? Are there tools you overuse?

▶ How comfortable are you with using all the technologies available to you?

▶ Where would you like coaching, training, or additional help? How will you get it?

Online Resources

If you would like some basic understanding of your communication style, and how to communicate better with others, you can take a free DISC assessment at:

LongDistanceTeammate.com/disc

For a tool to help you use insights from the DISC model to better communicate as part of a remote team, register at the website:

LongDistanceTeammate.com/resources

and request the **DISC Tool**.

Chapter 8

Creating Ethical Visibility

Sara knows she's being petty when her name gets left off a congratulatory email to the team. She knows she does good work, and she's positive that her manager simply forgot to include her. Still, it bothers her and makes her feel like she's invisible to her boss and her colleagues. Don't they know how hard she works and how much she brings to the table? The last thing she wants is to be seen as vain—or worse, needy—but being ignored or devalued is demoralizing, and she's wondering if it's not time to look for work elsewhere.

We've already established that one of the unintended consequences of working apart from your manager and your teammates is that you are often "out of sight and out of mind."

On your best days, this means you're not being interrupted all the time, and you're not being micromanaged or overloaded with tasks. The flip side of that is you often feel ignored. Are you being considered for that promotion or that special project? Did you get asked for your input on that question? Why were you the last person to hear about that problem? It can feel like you are invisible.

The dilemma is a common one: you want to be thought of as valuable and important to the workings of the team, without seeming like you need more attention than everyone else or drawing unwanted (and undeserved) attention to yourself.

How do you make yourself visible in a positive way to your manager and your teammates without seeming to make everything about you or coming across as vain or egotistical? We call this balancing act "Ethical Visibility."

What Is Ethical Visibility?

We're not talking about being a backstabbing bragger or claiming credit or attention that isn't due. It is a good thing to check things off your task list and get your work done. It's okay to attain your career and personal development goals. Nobody cares about those more than you do. And there's nothing wrong with wanting the appropriate rewards and recognition for your hard work and results. When you work remotely, or aren't in the office full time, you might not feel like you're getting your share of the credit.

No matter what you've been told in your life, your work will not speak for itself. You are your own best advocate, and Ethical Visibility is not "Hey, look at me, look at me, look how hard I worked. Look what a good teammate I am." It demonstrates all of that, but that doesn't mean you are standing on a soapbox and shouting. Ethical Visibility is about making sure that your work is recognized in the context of the team's work and results.

Ethical Visibility is:

- *About the team's/organization's goals, not you.* Make sure that you're using words like "we" and "us." When making suggestions, put them in the context of what the group is trying to achieve, not how smart you are. "Because the goal is to get more people to use this feature, maybe we can try using more testimonials" accomplishes the same thing as "I think we should use more social media" but makes the goal about the team, not your ego.

- *Appropriate to the team culture.* Some teams engage in raucous discussions that can get loud and boisterous. Other organizations are concerned with team cohesion and being "collegial" at all times, which might, to some, feel like avoiding conflict and quashing honest conversation. Being ethically visible means that you stand your ground and contribute but don't do it in a way that creates unnecessary tension or conflict within the team. For example, if things are usually done in writing, perhaps filibustering a meeting on another topic isn't the right way to be heard.

- *Supportive and positive.* Be aware of others and their feelings—and how you might be impacting them. It's good that everyone has ideas, even if not everyone's ideas are good. Being right or having a discussion in the heat of the moment may strain relationships. Even if you don't agree with some-one's contribution or idea, remember to focus feedback on the idea itself, not the teammate's intelligence or motives. We'll talk more about that in a future chapter.

- *Judged by behavior, not intent.* This is hard to hear, but just because you didn't mean to be rude to Alice might not mean she doesn't think you were rude. We can't always control how our actions are perceived by others. Getting defensive and saying, "Well, I was doing it for the good of the team" is irrelevant if the team thinks you were being pushy or disrespectful. Take feedback from others on how they want to be communicated with. Apologize for your actions, not how they were perceived. Remember this is harder when you work remotely from your teammates. Realize that being visible to your teammates is critical, and resolve to continually work at this.

Ethical Visibility and Your Boss

When building a solid relationship with your manager, it's important to remember two things. First, you are not the only person they're thinking about. Obvious as this is, you likely spend more time worrying and thinking about your manager than they spend pondering what you're up to. Wayne had a teacher once who said "Mr. Turmel, you don't want my undivided attention." And he was right. This means you need to be (ethically) visible enough to your boss that they keep you in mind and that they smile when they do.

Second, it is at least half your responsibility to manage and nurture the relationship and all your responsibility to influence their perception. You need to be around when needed and remind them in the most positive way of the value you bring to the team and how much you are engaged.

Here's what that means when it comes to working with your manager:

- *Participate in meetings and discussions when you can.* One of the few times you are together with both your leader and your teammates is during meetings. Whether conference calls, Skype meetings, or something else, this is your chance to demonstrate positive interaction with your peers, the ideas you bring to the table, and your commitment to the organization, the team, and your career. If you sit quietly answering email instead of contributing to the discussion or log on and tune out so nobody knows you're there, you are not likely to hit their radar screen.

Remember: If your manager is leading the meeting, there is a lot going on in her head. She will remember those who helped the team achieve their goals, and those who were perceived as roadblocks. Those who sit quietly and don't fall into either camp won't get much mindshare. Sometimes that's a blessing, but if you're invisible too much of the time, you can't be surprised if you are not top of mind.

- *Volunteer for assignments and projects.* Many remote workers complain that they are overlooked in favor of people who are in the same location as the manager. You may worry that when it's time for the boss to delegate tasks or seek assistance, you don't get considered. At first, this may seem great— you can keep your head down and not get extra work. But that's not in your best, long-term interest. During your one-on-one sessions, let your manager know the kinds of tasks you'd like to assist with, whether it's just to help or for your professional development (or both).

- *Offer to share what you know and learn.* One of the most powerful ways you can assist is by offering to share your expertise. This doesn't have to be a formal teaching event, although it could be. More importantly, be of assistance to anyone on the team—including your boss—who may be struggling with a process, or if the manager takes note of something you do well, offer to help others.

  You may have noticed that just because someone is the manager, doesn't mean they know how to do everything as well as the other team members. This is often true when it comes to technology and other details of your job. Politely offer to share your best practices or coach your boss through a piece of software or process. No matter where you are, you can be of assistance.

- *Own your personal and professional development.* Nobody should care about your personal development more than you. Yet, in many companies, it seems like yearly personal development plans are created then never mentioned again until the end of the year. It's not that your manager doesn't care; they just won't always have it in the front of their mind during your one-on-one conversations. The point isn't to blame them, but to take responsibility and accountability for what you need.

One of the most common challenges for remote leaders is ensuring that calls with their remote employees include both current tasks, and forward-looking discussions. When time is tight, and the manager is stressed, the conversations often become very task focused and transactional. When this happens, meetings devolve into an exercise of checking off boxes so that both of you can move on to the next thing on your lists. It's understandable, but that means the responsibility for these more personal, long-range conversations rests with you. If you don't raise the topic, it likely won't be discussed often enough.

- *Write down questions before coaching sessions so you don't forget.* Most one-on-one conversations are driven by your boss. They have a list of things to discuss, and limited time. Being human, they may be focused on getting through everything on their list. Yet you probably have questions that you want answered or wonder when that next learning opportunity or exciting project is coming your way. Don't assume that just because they didn't raise it, it's unimportant or they don't care. Help yourself and your manager by asking those questions or raising those concerns.

Here's the thing. Just as the leader's thoughts are often elsewhere during the call, yours may be too. How often have you hung up from a call and thought, "Oh no, I forgot to mention _____?" Own the discussion—and don't simply leave it to the leader or blame them when something important to you doesn't come up in the conversation. Keep a running list of questions ranging from the tactical to the big picture. Refer to your development plan and past calls to refresh your memory and bring them to the top of your mind.

Because we are both older, we have notebooks or journals that we track our calls and notes in, and we keep a running list of topics for the other person that is constantly updated. You can do the same thing by keeping an electronic file on your desktop that has notes from past calls, your development plan, and questions you wish to tackle on the next call. Take five minutes before each conversation to get centered and prepared. You're not being a pest; you are helping make your conversations more valuable and productive—and your leader will appreciate it.

Ethical Visibility with Your Teammates

How do your teammates know what you're doing, how hard you're working, how much you have their back, how much you care, and how engaged you are?

Here are some ways to be visible to your teammates:

- *Participate in meetings and projects.* If you are always silent, it's hard to show the value you bring to the team.

- *Contribute off-line as well as on.* Not everyone is comfortable speaking up in meetings, and if you work in a different time zone from your peers, it might be impossible to always contribute in the moment. But there are plenty of ways to make your presence felt in a positive way. Post to asynchronous tools, like Q & A forums, and instant message channels. Share learning and best practices with your teammates.

- *Send congratulatory notes when someone gets recognized for their good work.* Even though you're not in a position of authority, your colleagues appreciate signs of support and camaraderie. And be specific when you reach out. What did Alice do particularly well? What do you appreciate about her work? Compliments are more authentic when they are as specific as possible.

- *Fill out profiles on email/collaboration tools.* Are you simply a name next to a dot on Microsoft Teams or Slack, or does your face remind people of the real person on the other end of the message?

- *Use your webcam.* People connect on a more personal level when they put a face to your name. The more they associate the real you with that name on the bottom of the email, the more attention they pay and respect they give your message. Remember that you can use your webcam even when others don't use theirs. It might inspire more people to have richer, more meaningful conversations. We have more to say about webcams in chapter 12.

Pause and Reflect

▶ Ask yourself, How have I made myself Ethically Visible this week?

▶ Were there times you could or should have spoken up or addressed your manager or coworkers?

▶ Where are you overdoing it and needing to scale back a bit?

Chapter 9

Building and Maintaining Relationships

When everyone still worked in the office, Lucy really enjoyed most of her teammates. She enjoyed the camaraderie and interaction with most everyone. And even though she didn't particularly like working with Hector, they made it work when paired on project work. But now that everyone is telecommuting, she is having trouble staying connected with people like she used to. And working with Hector? Well, that hasn't gotten better either! Perhaps hardest of all, she doesn't even really know the new people from the other region that she must work with more now. And the new hires? She can't even keep their names straight.

Just because you are by yourself while you work in your home office, at the dining room table, or somewhere else doesn't mean that you are working alone. We've talked in chapter 6 about this fact from a work expectation and task perspective, but now we are talking about relationships. You are part of at least one team, even if you don't see people except on their profile photo or occasionally on the webcam. And since we are humans and not robots, we will (and must) interact. Since that is true, whether we are introverts or extroverts, relationships matter in getting your work done.

Why Relationships Matter

Let's be more specific about why relationships are important. There are organizational, interpersonal, and personal reasons. Here are some of the most important benefits you will gain as your relationships with your coworkers improve:

- *People do the work.* And when we know those people and understand their situation, strengths, weaknesses and faults, and hot buttons, we will work with them more effectively.

- *Communication improves.* You know it is easier to communicate with people that you know. When you know who they are, and even how they might respond in each situation, you can be more effective at getting your message received. And since communication is important and already hindered at a distance, investing in relationships is valuable.

- *Trust grows.* The whole next chapter is about trust, but for now, time spent building and maintaining relationships will build this important factor at work.

- *Stress and conflict are reduced.* Since we don't want more of these things (you might have enough of them in your life already), building relationships is like taking vitamins to help maintain a positive work experience.

- *Work is faster and easier.* When people know, like, and trust us, we will have stronger relationships. We respond quicker, put more effort into the communication, and enjoy working with those folks. Who doesn't want that?

- *Job satisfaction improves.* Hundreds of studies show what we already know: we like our work better when we like the people we work with. Increasingly, we find our friends at work. And as our work moves remote (like yours has), this will become more challenging. Working remotely is already isolating; doing it when we don't have a support system makes it even harder.

- *Organizational results improve.* All the "soft" reasons we've listed lead to one thing—better work output and productivity (there's that 3P Model again!). While "getting along" isn't all we need for great organizational results, it will amplify the strategy, the priorities, the goals, and all of the "harder" skills in the workplace.

Here's our belief: *relationships with others matter when you work remotely—maybe even more than when you see people every day.*

We have two more goals for this chapter. We want to:

- Guide you in overcoming the hurdles of distance in building and maintaining relationships

- Give you specific actions you can take

But before we go any further, we must address the elephant in the room . . .

Are We Talking Friendships?

No, we aren't talking about friendships really. Besides, even if we were, ten people have ten different definitions of the word. (Hey! I have 613 friends on Facebook!) Consider the following:

- Most people have teammates who they consider real friends. Research from Olivet Nazarene University shows that 82 percent of people say they have a friend at work, the average person has five friends at work, and 29 percent would describe a coworker as a best friend.[1]

- Work friendships may be just as strong as purely social ones, though more complicated. In a study led by Jessica R. Methot of Rutgers University across multiple companies in multiple industries, they found that when coworkers are also friends, while work might be more emotionally taxing, those same friendships can make us far more productive. "Workplace friends influence performance over and above purely instrumental or pure friendship-based relationships," the authors write.[2]

We aren't talking about friendships in this chapter (we aren't creating a new Remote Work Commandment: *Thou Shalt Make Friends at Work*), but building strong working relationships is our goal. And, if you become friends, perhaps all the better.

Relatedness and Interaction

We have different kinds of relationships in our lives—including our work lives. How we distinguish what type of relationship it is (and also how to build or change it) depends on two dynamics:

- Level of relatedness—how much do we have in common?

- Level of interaction—how often, and how, do we communicate?

    When you put them together, you get something like this (see figure 4):

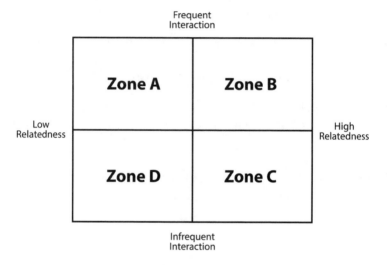

Figure 4. Relationship types

    You could take different people in your life and plot them in this matrix—in fact, we recommend that you do that. (We've provided a way to access a download of it at the end of the chapter if you want more space or if you are listening or reading electronically.) When you do that plotting, whether on paper or in your head, ask yourself:

- Where on this scale are the people I work with most closely?

- Where is my leader/manager?

- What is the balance of people that I see occasionally in the office and those I'm completely distant from?

And given the value of relationships at work, what does that tell you about the current state of yours today?

Take another look at these two factors and the implications when we work remotely. When compared to working with people in the same location, we have to work harder to find relatedness, and the frequency of our interaction likely drops.

And...

Neither of those need to be true.

Even if you don't have time or a desire to change your level of relatedness with an individual (though we would urge you to reconsider that), you can improve the relationship by increasing the interaction. In other words, you can move from Zone D to Zone A, or from Zone C to Zone B—it is in your control.

This requires the choice to be proactive in building your remote relationships and consider the long-term potential—and there is the 3P Model again.

Improving Working Relationships

Leaving our remote location out of the equation for a second, if we asked you to make a list of behaviors that would build or maintain working relationships, you could do that—and chances are your list would include things like:

- Care about the other person.

- Be a good listener.

- Offer to help when you can.

- Make time for them.

- Trust people.

- Make conversation about nonwork topics.

This proves that you know this stuff already. You didn't need us to talk to you about it, really. And yet, each of these things can be harder to do at a distance, if we think about them at all. So, if you used to work with someone and now you're working apart, you already had the relationship; some of these things you might continue to do naturally. But most of this doesn't come to us naturally when we're working from our own space. You're trying to do your work, working on your to-do list; you're not thinking about it this way. Let's talk about how to do that when we are remote, and not in the next cubicle or down the hall.

- *Make it a priority.* We know. You're busy. If you want to build and maintain relationships, though, you've got to make the effort. One of the mistakes that remote team members make is they don't think about themselves as being on a remote *team*. The title of this book is *The Long-Distance Teammate*, not *The Remote Worker*. You are in this with others, so make relationships a priority and be proactive in this area. If you go into the office or into the work space, you're going to (unless you are really introverted) naturally interact with people. But if you're working from home, you don't have those natural, spontaneous moments. You must make it a priority and decide this is part of your job.

- *Use multiple communication channels.* We've already talked about communication when working remotely and discussed the various tools you have at your disposal. If you want to invest in and build working relationships, you need to recognize that you need to use more of the tech at your disposal than just what you're used to. It means not simply doing what you think is the easiest or most expedient. If your job is more than just completing tasks, then it is time to do more than just fire off emails. You will build relationships faster and more effectively with the richer tools—more webcam and less email is a good starting point. This leads to our next piece of advice.

- *Make time for conversation.* Remember to chat with and check in with people, including those you might see in person occasionally. You must make time for this, and if you're not thinking about it as a remote teammate, it likely won't happen spontaneously. Plug some time into your calendar for when you're going to have the phone conversation or the webcam conversation. Take a couple of minutes to check in with the person, seeing what's going on with them. In the office you sat down sometimes and had coffee with people, or went to lunch together, right? You can still do those things. Get your coffee or sandwich, and turn on your webcam. It might need to be more planned than if you were in the same location, but you can still do it! Please note that we aren't saying to have idle chatter for an hour. The work is still the overall context—but maintaining those relationships is part of the work too.

- *Listen.* If you want to improve any relationship, improve your listening skills. If you are only sending emails, you're aren't listening in ways that build relationships, so be thinking about your communication options. But even so, you're still "listening" to emails too. Are you just trying to process them as quickly as you can? (Scanning them, anyone?) Or are you stepping back to make sure that you're thinking about that sender, to understand where they're coming from, and doing your best to understand their message? It Takes a little more discipline to do this at a distance, but it's to our advantage to do that. You know how to listen, so do it more intentionally and proactively.

- *Ask more questions.* One of the ways you can be a better listener is by asking more questions. We ask questions for at least three important purposes.

  - *Exploration.* As you listen to what people are saying (this could apply to text-based communication media too), ask follow-up questions to learn more or explore the topic in a deeper way. Sure, this helps you understand and learn, but it also lets the other person know that you care about them as well as their message.

  - *Understanding.* Ask questions to make sure you understand. Think about this as a sender rather than a receiver. You've been there—you are talking, and you don't feel like they really got what you meant. They didn't really ask any questions to clarify—so you sort of hope they got it, but you don't really know. When you are the receiver, don't do that to people! Asking things like "Is this really what you meant?" or saying "Tell me a little bit more about . . ." will improve clarity and understanding and build the relationship at the same time.

- ► *Connection.* Once you know what people are passionate about, you can ask questions about that. Wayne knows Kevin is a big Purdue sports fan, so he pays enough attention to ask a question about the game or commiserate if the outcome wasn't so great. Kevin recently had a conversation with a colleague at our publisher. He knows that person's daughter is a big-time high school volleyball player. So, he took a couple of minutes in the conversation, actually opening the conversation by asking about the volleyball team's season, and the conversation blossomed. For two or three minutes, they talked about volleyball. And then got down to business.

  When you're willing to take the time to ask questions and then listen, you are building relationships in those moments with those decisions. We think about questions as tools for communication, which they are. And yet when we do these things well, it changes how people perceive us, and helps us build relationships.

- ■ *Know what they are working on.* When you see people all day long, you likely know projects that they're working on. Once you are working remotely, you might not know those things. We aren't talking about being the nosy coworker. Pay attention to their weekly reports and look for other clues. You might even say, "Hey, I'm not trying to be nosy. I just want to make sure I know what's going on so I can be helpful if I can." You can't support someone, even with a "Hope it's going great" kind of conversation, unless you know what *it* is. Taking a little time to understand and know what others are working on helps both of you in many ways. It is hard to be supportive if you don't know what they might need. Be supportive; be willing and able to offer help.

- ■ *Build interaction, not transaction.* You've done or experienced this a thousand times. The phone rings and this is the conversation: "Hey, I need this help. Oh, okay, that is great. Thanks for the help." *Click.* That's a transaction. Remember this point: when you're working remotely, communications tend to become more transactional. To be the successful remote teammate you clearly want to be, you want to transcend as many communications as possible, taking them from transactional to interactional. In fact, if you would remember the phrase "I'm trying to create interactions, not transactions," you'll be heading in the right direction for building better remote relationships.

How can you build interactions and not transactions? Ask yourself, How do I make sure that at the end of our conversations, people feel it was worth their time, and they feel valued?

We're not talking about coddling people either, because I can hear some of you saying, "Guys, I've got work to do." Of course, there will be times when a phone call or email exchange will be direct, to the point, and transactional. Just don't let all of them devolve to that lower standard or relationships will be damaged.

- *Let them into your world.* We are talking about proactively, intentionally, building relatedness here. Yes, you can ask about them, but you must let people into your world as well. Some people have tight boundaries, and other people have wide boundaries in relation to what they care to share about themselves (and know about others).

- *Find the right boundaries.* While we aren't suggesting you have no limits on what you share, if you aren't willing to share very much, your relationships will suffer. If all you ever talk about with people is the work and maybe the weather, you don't have much chance to build a connection and relate to that person. When you're willing to share, once in a while, a little bit about your hobbies, a little bit about what you did on the weekend, it will make a difference—and open the door for the other person to do the same. This is how we find commonality and build relatedness.

It doesn't have to (and shouldn't) be a thirty-minute conversation every time you talk, but as people get to know you, it helps them work with you to build those connections. And again, so often in the office it happens because we're at the coffee machine or waiting for the microwave in the break room. Those spontaneous, serendipitous moments won't happen once you are remote. Do what you know to do, and apply it in a virtual, remote setting. Find the right boundaries for yourself and for them. Don't try to impede it. Don't try to "get all up in their business" if they aren't comfortable or interested, but work to find a balance that works for you and others.

- *Assume positive intent.* Assuming positive intent means that when we don't know what someone is doing, or know why they communicated something, we assume their intentions were honorable, above board, and for the good of others. Building the habit of starting with this initial assumption will help you in all relationships, but especially when you're working remotely.

When you are in a different location, you can't see what people are doing, or always know what is really going on—so you make assumptions. Our colleague, Guy Harris, says that "we ought to at least assume benign intent, which means that they're not doing something to us. They're just doing stuff. Recognize they weren't even thinking about what it did to us." While we agree with Guy, we are suggesting going beyond benign intent and assuming their motives are positive.

Of course, it is possible that their intent is more nefarious. It's also possible that they're not thinking about you in the least. But if we start with positive intent—you believe others are trying to do good work for good reasons. They're not trying to screw you over. They're not trying to do stuff to hurt you. It is all an assumption anyway, right? How often do you really know someone's intent? You can't "know" unless they tell you—and even then, it might not be the truth.

You are sitting at home, working by yourself, and the pronoun in your head is *they*. *They* did this; *they* said that. *They* don't care. *They* were being sloppy. Whether you're talking about a single person or about a whole group of people, the more that you're using *they* language, the more likely you will move to the cynical, negative-intent assumptions. None of that starts with an assumption of positive intent.

We are challenging you to stop thinking *they* and start thinking *John*, and *Josh*, and *Joan*, and *Jan*, and *José*. The more that you think about people by their first name and as individuals—the less often you will move to negative intent. If you don't, you become more insular and less likely to think like a teammate.

Until you have more information, assume the best. When you do, you will have less stress and worry and will improve trust, communication, and your relationships.

- *Go first.* As you read this section, you may be thinking that some other people on your team need to read this book—they need to do these things. That may be true, and you could, after all, buy them a copy. But don't point the finger away from yourself here. We are suggesting that you go first. Remember that second "P" in the 3P Model is *proactivity.*

  You can be the one that goes first to build the relationship. Others might not see what you now see—that when we have better working relationships, our work is easier, is more fun, and will drive better results. Once you have that mindset, you can start. Others don't even have to agree with you at first. You can break the ice. Just start, because waiting won't improve relationships. You'll be amazed what happens when you open the doors to having a quick phone call. Ask more questions about what's going on with other people, about their work, and about their life outside of work. You'll be amazed at how things will start to change.

Remember, you already know how to do this. You've done it all your life. We're just now doing it with more intention, more proactively, and with the belief that we can build great relationships even if we are remote from each other.

Pause and Reflect

▶ Who do you most need to focus on building your relationship with?

▶ Which actions will give you the most immediate impact?

▶ Which actions might be harder? How can you do them even if they are hard?

Online Resource

To download the Relationship Types Matrix and a tool to help you use it, register at the website:

LongDistanceTeammate.com/resources

and request the **Relationship Types Matrix**.

Chapter 10

Building and Maintaining Trust

Kofi is new to this project team. While everyone has been friendly enough, it seems like the half of the team working in the office stick together and tend not to reach out to him. Those working elsewhere have been more welcoming, but he speaks to only a few on a regular basis, and when he has a question, those are the people he asks rather than the people in the office. Lately his manager has been asking for more updates than usual and Kofi's wondering if there's something going on that he's unaware of.

The paradox of working remotely is that it requires a lot of trust—you need to rely on people to make things happen, and they need to rely on you, yet you seldom see each other. When it works, it works well. The problem is, when working remotely, trust is far more fragile.

Trust and the 3P Model

Trust directly impacts, and is impacted by, the 3Ps. Let's look at each of them:

- *Productivity.* It is difficult to work as quickly or as effectively if you will go to only certain people for information, or if you have to constantly check Bob's work because "you know how he is."

  As a teammate, you need to step up more often and take the initiative in communication. That's not always easy to do, but trust makes communication work. Think about trust as both an accelerant—things can get done faster—and a lubricant—they will be easier. When greater trust exists, you are more likely to be proactive in reaching out to others. You have faith in the information people send you and don't do as much double-checking and verifying. As trust grows between you and your teammates, so does your productivity.

- *Proactivity.* How proactive we are greatly influences the level of trust.

  Here's a simple example: when you're not constantly double-checking, when you're not waiting for more data, when you believe what you hear the first time, you act faster and there are fewer misunderstandings. If you've got somebody that you exchange emails with and you're always second-guessing their intent, or it sounds like they're in a bad mood today, it impacts your ability to act assertively, and maybe even your willingness to engage at all.

- *Potential.* Of course, since we work better and more positively with people we trust (and vice versa), the little things that sow seeds of doubt may have long-term—potential—bad effects.

The Problem with Mistrust

The opposite of trust is mistrust, and it can make work less enjoyable and harder. When trust is low, you're suspicious of people's motives—"I guess I've got to work with Alice on this." When people don't trust each other, they aren't proactive about reaching out and so communication bogs down. Then we disengage—there's less interaction on the team, so we focus on our own tasks and work.

If we have not proven ourselves trustworthy, we may miss out on opportunities for recognition and promotion. Over time, that can damage the way we feel about our work and teammates.

How do you know that there's mistrust on a team? Here are some clues—and you might not even think about them as trust issues:

- *Duplication.* There's a lot of copying each other on emails, and the boss gets cc'd often. If you find yourself copying the manager on everything that you do with Alice, because she doesn't seem to respond unless you drag your manager into it, it's a giant red flag that trust is an issue on your team.

- *Rework and delay.* There's a lot of resending stuff over and over because you don't believe that they downloaded it or read it the first time. When we work remotely, we don't often communicate with each other as well as we might. And when we do, it's not necessarily positive. Having to constantly double-check work or follow up on communication just to make sure it was received slows down the work and can erode trust over time.

- *Gossip.* There's a lot of talk after meetings. People get with their buddy and say, "Hey, what's going on there? What do you think they really meant?"

- *Exclusion.* There's one behavior that we don't even notice. People are excluded because it seems easier. It's just simpler not to copy Larry in Accounting on that memo. "Bob doesn't really know much about this anyway, so I'm going to ask only these ten team members for help or for information."

The Trust Triangle

In *The Long-Distance Leader,* we shared a model with leaders that applies no matter who you are, or what your place on the team is (figure 5).

Figure 5. The Trust Triangle

Trust contains three components. You need to have a *common purpose*. You need to believe in the other person's *competence* and their *motives*. If any of these is lacking, we can lose faith in our teammates. On the other hand, the more proof we have, the more we trust our colleagues. This is true of any relationship. Let's look at each component briefly:

- *Common purpose.* Is everyone doing things for the same reasons? Are we all rowing in the same direction? A common purpose is probably the least affected by distance. The company has a mission, purpose, and vision. Those can be communicated pretty effectively remotely. Generally, we do a decent job being aware and aligned.

  Sometimes it's easier than others. If you're a contractor, for example, not an employee, that can be an issue. If you're on a project team where you have a project manager, but you also have a "real boss" somewhere that you have to answer to, you might be seen as not aligned. If people don't believe you have the same priorities as everybody else, or that you're not giving enough time to one or the other, trust suffers.

- *Competence.* This is directly impacted by distance because you don't see your peers every day. Let's say you've known Helen forever. You used to work in the office together. She doesn't say much in meetings, but she takes a lot of notes and you know that she's really engaged and really good at her job.

  Then there's Larry in Denver. Larry's new to the team. You've met him maybe once. He never says anything during meetings, and he seldom contributes to online discussions. If you have a question, who are you going to go to? If you keep going to Helen and never go to Larry, what's he going to think? That you don't trust him—so chances are he won't trust you either . . . It's not that Larry isn't good at his job, it's just that you don't have a lot of evidence to know. If Larry misses one appointment, you might make a bigger deal out of it than you would with someone whose work you know better.

  We build our opinion of people's competence, and they build theirs about us, based on the evidence at hand. If they don't have any evidence, that's a pretty flimsy structure to build trust on.

- *Motives.* We also look for proof of people's motives. Larry might be good at his job, but does he care? Does he have your back? If you send out a request for help and Mary answers right away and gives you great information, but you don't hear from Bob until the end of the day, what does that mean? Bob got to it when he got to it, or it might mean that Mary has your back and Bob doesn't care if you live or die. Which is it?

There may be conflict between people's personal work and their responsibility for the team. Larry's really good at his job, but he doesn't participate in team stuff because he's worried only about his own work. That may or may not be true. When we don't have enough evidence, our brain tends to make stuff up and we rarely make up the best-case scenario. When we suspect other people's motives and when they suspect ours, nothing good happens. There's a lot of double- and triple-checking, and gossip starts.

When we trust other people, social reciprocity grows. It means I trust you exactly as much as you trust me. If you go out of your way to demonstrate that you're good at your job and you care, it's simply good manners, and human nature, for me to do the same for you. If we're engaged and positively working together, trust tends to build and build and build. If you offer enough proof of purpose, competence, and motives, you'll have an enhanced image and impact. It's part of that Ethical Visibility. If people think positively about us, they're going to trust us. It creates a more pleasant work environment.

If somebody looks like they're working under bad information or somebody is struggling with something and you've got a moment, odds are better you'll help without being asked. When that happens, you're seen, not just as a contributing member of the team, but as a truly great teammate.

The problem over time is that our evidence needs updating. We may start out trusting Bob, but it doesn't take much to shake that. Are you providing evidence that you care? Are you providing evidence that you're good at your job? Are you giving status updates that tell people truly how well things are going? Do you step up without being asked? That's how you provide evidence.

We build our mental database through our interactions, and many of those involve technology. We can't watch people in their cubes if they're on the other side of the country, so we look at their chat discussions, phone calls, webcam calls, and meetings. Those are synchronous tools—everyone involved is participating at the same time.

Not everybody is comfortable speaking up on a conference call, though. Good thing there are asynchronous tools as well: Slack, Jabber, Microsoft Teams, whatever you're using for chat discussions. Good asynchronous communication can include online questions and answers, especially if you work across time zones.

When you work in different time zones, asynchronous tools can be great trust builders. These tools require proactivity—if you answer only when asked, it will have an impact on how people in your team and organization view you.

You need to be honest about the level of trust on your team and in your organization. Do you feel micromanaged? Do you feel supported?

For this to happen, of course, you need to provide evidence that you are trustworthy. That goes back to being ethically visible, not being a showboat, and demonstrating your alignment, competence, and motivation.

If you're not entirely comfortable reaching out, one technique is to offer an explanation and context for requests. "Bob, I'm asking you this not because I want to add to your workload, but because you're the guy on this particular topic." Explaining why you're seeking input can go a long way to removing doubts about how and why you're communicating.

By applying the 3P Model, you can intentionally build trust. This will help you get your work done, build healthy relationships, and make your work more enjoyable.

Pause and Reflect

▶ What evidence of purpose, competence, and motives do you require from others?

▶ How will you provide those to help others build trust in you?

Online Resource

To use a tool to better understand the level of trust in your working relationships, register at the website:

LongDistanceTeammate.com/resources

and request the **Trust Tool**.

Chapter 11

Giving and Receiving Feedback

Feedback wasn't always plentiful when Norma worked in the office, but occasionally there was some simple acknowledgment from her teammates in the hallway. Now that she is working from home? Nothing. She is deafened by the silence, and without feedback she is left wondering about how she is doing. She is operating under the "no news is good news" theory, but is unsure if that is accurate, and she'd really like to know.

A lot has been written about giving feedback as a leader, supervisor, or coach, and we've written some of it. Far less has been written about giving feedback as a peer or teammate. And unfortunately, even less is written about the other side of the feedback coin—receiving it.

Like Norma, most remote workers receive even less feedback than they did when in the office. And chances are, they weren't getting enough then either. Now all they hear are crickets.

Yes, we need feedback from the boss (and leaders who are reading, we aren't letting you off the hook here), but as a coworker, you have a valuable perspective too. And if you are trying to become a more valuable, more engaged, and more connected member of the team, feedback is a good place to step up.

What Is Feedback, Anyway?

The most relevant definition of *feedback* on Dictionary.com is this.

Psychology. **knowledge of the results of any behavior, considered as influencing or modifying further performance.**[1]

Imagine this scenario. You and several of your teammates, all peers, are in a virtual meeting, and you happen to mention that you need to give Sandra some feedback. What is everyone else thinking about Sandra and your upcoming "feedback"? They all wonder what Sandra did wrong, and they are glad they aren't Sandra at this moment.

Ken Blanchard may call feedback "the breakfast of champions," but that is not how most people define it. Don't believe us? Imagine how you would feel if on Friday your leader told you she wanted to give you some feedback on Monday morning. Are you looking forward to *that* breakfast?

Look back at the definition again. Notice that there isn't a mention of whether it is positive or negative. The word *feedback* is neutral, even though that isn't how most of us think about it.

Most people do receive more negative than positive feedback at work, and by our estimation that ratio can be even worse when the work is done remotely. Leaders often wait to give feedback until there's a "good reason." Unfortunately, the motivation is rarely for good performance.

As a committed, engaged member of a team, don't you want "knowledge of the results of any behavior, considered as influencing or modifying further performance"? Don't you want to know when you are doing great, so you can keep doing those things? And don't you want to know if you are falling short and need to improve?

We all do.

At least people like you definitely do. And don't the teammates that are most effective and enjoyable to work with want that too?

For sure.

Is This Part of My Job?

We know, you are likely thinking this isn't your job. After all, isn't that why the boss gets the big dollars and does the performance review? We aren't absolving your boss of their role, just challenging you to think about yours a bit differently.

Remember the 3P Model? If you want to be engaged, connected, and successful while working remotely, each of the Ps apply here:

- *Productivity.* If you help people keep doing great things (positive feedback) and avoid or correct mistakes or weaknesses (negative feedback), are you helping them improve your productivity? Is it helping the team overall? And selfishly, won't their success help you be more productive too?

- *Proactivity.* Being willing to give people input to help them, when it isn't in your job description and might even be uncomfortable to do so, is almost the definition of being proactive. You don't have to. No one is expecting you to. But when you do it well (we're getting there), it can make a positive difference for everyone.

- *Potential.* No one can reach their potential on their own. Everyone needs coaching, whether formal or informal. If you give feedback, you help people move toward their potential. And, because of the principle of reciprocity, the best chance you have of getting this feedback yourself is by giving it, and then receiving it graciously.

Besides, being a teammate means caring enough about your peers to help them succeed, and possibly even help them get more positive feedback from the boss. After all, if you give your teammates a fresh perspective and help them improve, perhaps you'll get more positive feedback from them in return.

In that case, everyone wins, right?

The Four Types of Feedback

Feedback isn't only negative, though we usually receive more negative feedback and tend to remember it longer. And if you think there is positive feedback and negative feedback, you are half right.

We think there are *four* types of feedback:

- *Negative feedback.* You know what this one is. Specifically, it's negative comments about something that happened in the past. It is about something that didn't go so well or could have gone better, in the past (e.g., "During the team call yesterday, Felipe, you interrupted others several times—and here is how that impacted the meeting").

- *Positive feedback.* This is positive comments about something that happened in the past. It is about something that did go well, in the past (e.g., "I appreciated how you paused after you made your point during your presentation yesterday, Felipe—it allowed others to share their ideas").

- *Negative feedforward.* This is comments about what to avoid or not to do in the future (e.g., "Whatever you do, Felipe, during your presentations, don't turn off your webcam or we won't be able to see your reaction").

- *Positive feedforward.* This is comments about what to do, or advice for what to do, in the future (e.g., "Felipe, when you take more time to prepare for meetings, you will get better results").

If you were thinking that this chapter was about giving (and receiving) only negative feedback, you would be wrong. While that may well be part of the conversation, it shouldn't be the only feedback you ever give!

Remember that whether the commentary is focused in the past or in the future, the purpose is to help people improve. We are encouraging our teammates to stop doing something, change something, or reinforce something they are doing well.

Look at the four types of feedback again. If our goal is to influence people to change or do something differently, we must have a balance of the four types. If you give only feed*back*, and speak only about the past, you are giving people a history lesson. Remember that you can't change the past. You will be a more effective influencer with your feedback if you put what happened with a plan to answer the practical "now what?" question.

The Psychology of Feedback

Let's leave the dictionary at the door and move to the real world of remote work. The goal of feedback is to provide people with information, data, or observations that will influence them to change their thinking and behavior for mutual benefit. For that to happen, feedback must be:

1. Heard

2. Understood

3. Accepted

4. Applied

As a teammate, you might be uncomfortable offering feedback (Is it really my place?), and others must be open to receiving it from you (Why is Jenni giving me feedback?). If the manager is giving feedback, we expect it as a part of the implicit agreement and expectations of work. And after all, because of their position, we will likely value it (even if we don't like it or we disagree with it).

Is it even possible to give feedback if we aren't the boss?

Think about it outside of work for a second. You are far more likely to follow the four steps (from heard to applied) if three factors are present. You are more open to feedback from someone if they . . .

■ *Have a position of power.* That's the boss, but also your mom, your spouse, the judge, and the police officer.

■ *Have credibility.* If you think or know that someone knows what they are talking about, you are far more interested in, and open to, their feedback or input. Think teammates with lots of experience.

■ *Have a relationship with you.* You will ask people in your life for feedback when you know they have your best interests at heart, right? Which of your teammates do you trust and believe wants the best for you?

Leaders automatically have the first one but must earn the other two. As a teammate you may already have the second two—meaning that your feedback is far more likely to be heard, understood, accepted, and applied by your peers than you might have thought. Especially if you do it well.

How to Give Feedback as a Teammate

Since you don't have the position of boss, how you give feedback to your teammates is exceptionally important. Remember you can lean on your perceived credibility and your existing relationship. This will likely leave them more open to your insights and feedback.

Building both of those can be harder when you work at a distance from those teammates you might want to give feedback to, but you have many new ideas and tools at your disposal now to help build your credibility and maintain relationships that support these conversations.

You still need to build the awareness and expectation that you have feedback and that your intent is positive and helpful (please, make sure it is, okay?). To do that, you must start with a question that asks permission to share your observations:

- Hey, can we talk about how meetings are going? I have some observations.

- Would you be open to some feedback on X?

- Would it be okay if I shared my perspective?

At first, until there is a pattern or an agreement to share with each other, you should ask. And if they say no, let it drop. Asking, getting a no, and then continuing anyway isn't going to go well—and likely you won't be heard.

Once you have agreement, here are a few tips to make the feedback you give more effective (and actually easier to deliver):

- *Make it a two-way conversation.* Try to understand their perspective on the situation first; don't just give them some feedback without their input.

- *Use the phone or the webcam*—please. You have a much better chance for success and are far more likely to be understood and have the message accepted than if it's just words in an email or a text.

- *Slow down.* Speed isn't necessarily your friend. You don't need a thirty-minute meeting, but blurting out your observations won't work very well either.

- *Stick to the facts.* Observations, not judgment, will help. When people feel judged, they shut down, and you likely won't even get to step 2. Remember, building and maintaining trust requires evidence.

- *Make it meaningful.* Talk about things that matter. The color of their blouse on the team call? It probably doesn't make that much difference.

- *Be specific.* Vague comments won't help. Share what you saw specifically. A generic "good job" isn't very helpful.

- *Be kind.* If you want to be helpful, start by being kind. As we have stated elsewhere in the book, you can be clear and kind. Make it clear you care about the person and their success.

- *Be timely.* Don't stew about it and wait forever. Give the feedback as soon as you are able to give it and they are ready to receive it.

Tips on Receiving Feedback Effectively

Receiving feedback can be hard, especially when what we are hearing is a negative surprise or people don't use all (or any!) of the advice from the previous section. Even if it is hard, recognize that one of the ways for the feedback you give to be better received is to be a better receiver yourself. Make sure you model the behaviors you'd like in return. Here are some tips to help you succeed:

- *Be open.* If you aren't open to the feedback, it won't go well. And remember, some of the feedback might be really good!

- *Dampen your defensiveness.* When your defensive armor goes up, the other person can tell, and you won't learn anything anyway. Try to keep your defenses down and your ears open.

- *Assume positive intent.* Even if their intent isn't always in your best interest, start by assuming it is, and look for the kernel or nugget that can help you.

- *Be curious.* Since you aren't being defensive, you can be curious and ask questions to explore and understand the feedback.

- *Make sure you understand.* Once you understand it, you are in a better position to apply it.

- *Thank them.* It is the gracious thing to do. And if you know their intent was honorable, and you remember how hard it might be to give feedback, you will realize how valuable it is to thank them for helping you with their perspective.

Final Thoughts

This might be the most valuable chapter in the book for you, especially if you haven't really considered your role as a teammate in the feedback process. So many of the other great things we are promoting and helping you achieve in this book can be advanced faster as you get good at these two skills.

Being a remote worker is very different from being a Long-Distance Teammate. Teammates care about their peers, about their results and success. And when they do, they take responsibility for helping them succeed. Giving feedback to them, and graciously receiving it, is one way to do this.

Pause and Reflect

► How comfortable are you with the idea of offering feedback to teammates? What has been your past experience?

► Where can you comfortably start giving feedback now?

► How can you be more effective in receiving feedback now?

Online Resource

We didn't have time to go deeply into how we all receive feedback and the steps we go through when we do. That is why we have created a tool to help you understand that process better as both a sender and a receiver of feedback. To access that tool, register at the website:

LongDistanceTeammate.com/resources

and request the **Stages of Feedback Tool**.

Chapter 12

How to Work with Others Remotely

When COVID-19 hit, Richard was looking forward to working from home more often. On the few occasions he'd done it before, he was able to accomplish a lot and felt productive. Now that he's permanently working remotely, he sometimes creates his own systems and ways of doing things, but he is no longer feeling as productive and has a harder time coordinating his work with the rest of his teammates'.

For most of us, one of the prime benefits of working remotely is that we can concentrate on our work better than when we are in an office environment. The problem is that for most of us to do great work, we need to work with other people.

In the traditional workplace, the rules and norms for how things get done are shared and demonstrated on a regular basis. You're often within a few steps of someone if you have a question or need help. If you don't know where to locate the Jackson file, you can just ask the person at the next desk.

That's not to say that working with others is ever easy, exactly, but experience has taught you how to make it work. When we are isolated from our teammates much (or all) of the time, this becomes—maybe not harder—but certainly more complicated. This requires you to be more mindful of how you interact and collaborate with your teammates and manager.

In many ways the other chapters in this part are all about working with others, but there are things outside of building relationships and trust, and communication and meetings, that still need to be shared.

There are three factors we haven't yet discussed that will help you work more effectively with others in a remote environment:

- Understanding the work that needs to be done so everyone is working toward the same goals.

- Knowing the tools, technology, and processes that make your team productive.

- Prioritizing tasks so you can be productive while balancing "your work" with "team work."

Understanding the Work

As we have said before—the work is more than "your work." Make sure you see the big picture and how you fit into it. It gives you context for the work and insight into who you're working with and how best to perform your job to those ends. You can do things in a mindful, intentional way if you have a broader view of the job in front of you.

To really understand the work, you must be able to answer these three questions:

- What is the work we're doing?
- What does success look like?
- Who are the stakeholders?

Let's start with understanding what the work is. The easiest part is knowing what needs to be done. If we know the tasks that need doing, and how they are to be done, we have a pretty good idea of what to do each day. For most of us, though, that's not enough. We need to know why the tasks are important. When you add up all that work, what are you and your teammates trying to accomplish?

For most people, context is critical to doing a good job. A few of us can take a task and simply run with it: "The boss told me to do it, and do it this way, so I'm doing it." Most people, though, want to understand the job at hand.

What are we trying to accomplish? Why is it important? What's the best way to accomplish it?

Timing is also important. When does this task need to be done? Do your teammates or customers have timelines that require your help? Getting something checked off your list seems less important if you can do a different task that helps a colleague meet a deadline. It's more satisfying, you build better working relationships, and the whole team is more productive if everyone isn't working on their own timeline.

The next part of understanding the work is to know when you've succeeded. If you say you've completed a task, but your manager says it's not good enough, or your teammates have to do a bunch of rework as a result of your efforts, you've performed a task but it certainly wasn't good work. Metrics matter, and when we work remotely and don't have immediate feedback on our work, they are crucial.

Many of us are familiar with SMART goals. There's lots of good information on this out in the world, but it is an acronym that stands for Specific, Measurable, Actionable, Realistic, and Timely. To really do a good job, you need to understand all five of these factors.

Here's an example. If you're told "Fill out this report," that might sound simple. But if it needs to be filled out in a certain way, by Friday afternoon, and you don't know that, you could fill it out incorrectly and get it in late. So you can complete the task in your mind but still not be successful. Sure, you did it, but it's not done right, and it can create all kinds of problems down the line for your manager and your teammates.

Understanding how your work will be measured is critically important to your productivity, motivation, and engagement. It's also your responsibility.

Wait. What? Isn't my manager supposed to tell me what she wants? Yes, it's important that you are given clear guidance, but it's up to you to make sure you understand your marching orders. Being proactive about understanding all the expectations and metrics of your job will heighten your chances of success and demonstrate how much you care.

So far, we've been focusing on the job you have to do as if it's a matter between you and your manager. But odds are you will rely on others for input or information, and others will have to work with the output of your efforts. That's why knowing the stakeholders helps you get the right work done in the right way.

Imagine you are standing in a river. Stakeholders are those people both upstream and downstream of your position. Work flows past you from upstream and continues downstream. The people who assign you tasks must be satisfied. Sometimes that person is an external customer who places an order, or it's an internal customer (your manager, Accounts Payable, whoever) who sets you a SMART goal or task. When you've completed it, your work product continues downstream. The order has to be filled, and if you haven't done your job, the poor person in shipping will not be able to do their job.

To get work done successfully, we have to understand the nature of the work. We must know what has made us successful, and who else is impacted. That way we can make smart decisions and complete our tasks in ways that truly add value to the team and our organization.

Knowing the Tools, Technology, and Processes That Make Your Team Productive

As we discussed in chapter 6 when talking about setting expectations, knowing *what* you're supposed to do is important, but especially when working remotely, we also need to know *how* it needs to be done. Teamwork depends on everyone working in concert, not each person doing things the way that works best for them individually.

In order to achieve at a high level, remote teams need agreement and common understanding on how the work will be done together. That means great teammates must:

■ Know which tools their team is expected to use.

■ Use those tools competently.

■ Follow established team processes or work with teammates to improve them.

Knowing Which Tools Your Team Is Expected to Use (and Then Using Them)

You can't survive in the working world today without using technology. When you are working remotely, it is critical that you become comfortable with it and know how to use it well. Using the wrong tool in the wrong way can create big problems, even if you are "doing your job."

Here's an example: you hate instant messaging. You much prefer to send emails because you can write longer, more detailed messages. So, you send a request for information to Alice and then sit waiting, drumming your fingers for a response. It seems to take Alice forever to respond to you. But there's an agreed-upon twenty-four-hour response time on emails—so that isn't her fault. If you wanted a response sooner, you should send the instant message, even though you don't like the tool, because she'd have gotten back to you sooner.

Yes, email works. Yes, you prefer it to something else. And, yes, if you stay with email because of your personal preference, you are messing with the way everyone else on the team is trying to get things done. If you really believe your method is best, don't just do your own thing, converse with the other members to ensure that you can all agree on how to get the work accomplished.

As a team, decide what tools to use under which circumstances and stick to it, even if it's not your preference. More about this in a minute.

Using the Tools Competently

Software engineers will tell you that most of us use only 20 percent of the available features of tools like Webex or Microsoft Teams. To make matters worse, we don't even use the same 20 percent.

If your job depended on using a piece of machinery, but you used only about a fifth of its capabilities, you'd either be working inordinately hard or be fired. Since you have a web meeting platform that has webcam capability, whiteboards, file transfer, and other features and you use it only for voice calls and instant messaging, it's no wonder work feels so difficult and communicating is such a challenge.

What tools do you and your team have at your disposal? Which ones are you leveraging, and which ones are you ignoring or not using well? It's not unusual for team members to have different levels of confidence and competence with technology. What's not okay is letting fear or a lack of confidence today interfere with your ability to work with others. That's a challenge that is yours to overcome.

Good teammates are proactive in offering to help others improve their skills. If you have knowledge or know a trick that not everyone knows, share it in a meeting or one on one so that the whole team is operating at the highest level possible.

It's okay to ask for help. Most people never get the real training they need on apps and software they use regularly. We've learned it by watching others or getting to know just enough to get our work done. Check with your manager and your teammates to get the coaching and help you need. Take training where it's available. And there is a YouTube video for just about everything. Not knowing your tools is one thing; choosing to remain hampered is a different, and the wrong, choice.

A Word about Webcams

No tool in your team's kit is better at building and maintaining communication and working relationships than webcams. Still, some people hate them and don't want to use them.

Because of the great value of webcams and sometimes strong negative reaction to them, we need to say more about this tool.

If there's one sea change that has occurred as a result of the COVID-19 boost in people working from home, it's the use of webcams. Many people who avoided using them in the past could no longer make excuses when the entire team was on several meetings a day.

There's a reason this happened. When getting together as a whole team was no longer possible, your teammates did what they could to compensate for the visual, in-person communication. The timing was also right, as tools such as Google Meet, Microsoft Teams, Zoom, and others removed many of the complicated technical barriers and quality issues to meeting in cyberspace.

Understand that our brains are trained to visually connect whenever possible. It makes sense: when we can see someone's eyes, read their facial expressions, and see their body language, we receive much more of the intended (and sometimes unintended) message—we can communicate much more effectively. In addition, there is something hardwired in us to instinctively connect to people we see face-to-face. Yet people consistently resist using the tool that will give us this human connection in a virtual world! Sometimes it's for valid reasons (they suck up a lot of bandwidth and can be problematic on VPNs) and sometimes the reasons are a bit, well, lame.

Here are some of the most common objections to using webcams, and how to get over them:

- *When I work from home, I look awful and don't want to be on camera.* Okay, take a shower and a breath. We're not telling you what your hygiene habits should be, but just because you're working from home doesn't mean that you should be a slob. Four or five days in, no shaving, no showering? Come on, now. This lackadaisical approach to yourself can negatively impact your focus and the way you approach your work. You don't need to be in a three-piece suit or a blouse and skirt (unless when you face your customers, that's how you dress). On days when you know you will be on camera, be presentable (whatever business casual is in your company), and remember, on webcam you need to be dressed only from the belly button up.

- *My office is a mess, or I don't want people to see I'm working on my dining room table.* We don't all have the perfect home office or working conditions. Many webcam platforms like Zoom and Microsoft Teams allow you to blur out your background or even have fancy templates so it looks like you're working in front of the Golden Gate Bridge. If that doesn't work for you, there are tools like the Webaround (http://TheWebaround.com), which is a collapsible screen that slides over the back of your chair and creates a neutral background while blocking out the disaster area that is the rest of your work space.

- *The lighting in my work space makes me look bad or puts me in the shadows.* It's not easy to connect to someone who looks all dim and shadowy, like the mystery witness in a crime documentary. Very few of us need professional-quality lighting when we're on webcam, but people want to be able to see your face. Make sure the light in front of you is brighter than the light behind you. You can do this by closing the curtains behind you if you have your back to a window or light source. Try flipping to the other side of the table when you are on camera. A simple solution Wayne used in his former office was a cheap thrift-store table lamp on his desk that he could turn on so the light was on his face during webcam calls; that way, people could see him.

■ *Really, I just hate seeing myself on camera.* When we work with clients around the world, people admit that while being able to see the other person is a huge advantage, they really hate seeing their own faces. Get over it. After you've used the webcam a few times, you become numb to the size of your pores or whatever else is bothering you. Most virtual meeting platforms allow for multiple ways of viewing the screen. Set it to speaker or presenter view so that you won't see everyone, just the person speaking. You'll be able to look at yourself less often. Finally, just understand the value that being able to see the other person brings to interactions and the role it plays in building relationships, and get over yourself.

All this use of cameras and meeting online has also created a new problem. The term "Zoom fatigue" has come into use. While these tools are terrific and allow us to replicate many of the benefits of meeting in person, they also work differently with our bodies.

Our eyes weren't meant to scan a brightly lit screen constantly. We can't resist looking at everyone's video, constantly scanning instead of focusing on one piece of information. It's physically draining to speak or focus without getting the kind of feedback that makes in-person meetings so rewarding, like laughter, smiles, and the energy of a crowd.

One way to avoid this is to change the view on your screen. Most platforms allow you to see everyone at once (usually called gallery view). You can also switch to speaker view, or active speaker view, which shows only the person speaking at that moment. It's easier on your eyes and brain.

This isn't to say you shouldn't use the tools at your disposal, but be mindful that too long in front of a screen is draining. Frequent short meetings are better than long ones, and webcams work best in one-on-one situations, and less well in large (over fifteen) groups.

Like every tool in your team's toolkit, check in with your teammates about what's working for you and what isn't.

Knowing and Following Team Processes

Every organization has work processes—right or wrong—and accepted ways of doing most of the work. When we work in the same location, those processes are often transparent and easy to pick up on—and if you have a question, there's always someone available to help you.

When you work on your own much of the time, you might not know how things should be done. If expectations aren't clear, or if you're new to the team, asking may feel awkward. But the alternative is trying to figure it out on your own—that isn't a good option either. Often remote workers are so focused on getting the work done individually that they are blind to, or don't even think about, the shared work processes. To their detriment, they become convinced that results matter more than process.

It can be tempting, if you don't like using a tool or you think a process is too slow, to find a workaround. Before you change how your work is done, ask yourself how that change might affect other stakeholders. If you do this fabulous report in Word, but they need it in another format, it doesn't really matter how good the content is. You've created a log jam for somebody else. Team processes matter.

When the way things get done doesn't seem to work, there are a couple of things to consider. First, do you understand both the process and why it is done that way? Talk to your peers and see if they share your pain. Then ask yourself what your objection is to the current process. Are your concerns legitimate or based on your personal preferences, biases, or discomfort?

If the problem lies with you, it's time to consider upgrading your skills. Maybe you need to watch some tutorials or take some training. Most likely, though, you'll have to take the proactive—and uncomfortable—step of asking for help from your manager or your peers. Great teammates understand what works best for the team and adjust their preferences when necessary. Sometimes you just have to suck it up.

Prioritizing Tasks to Balance Your Work with Team Tasks

Scheduling and prioritizing work is one of the hardest things about working remotely. How do you decide what's important and what's not? How do you determine what gets done and what is put off until tomorrow? Some of the ways we prioritize make perfect sense:

- Tasks with specific deadlines

- Customer-facing duties

- Urgent requests from teammates

- Assignments from your manager

We are sure you agree, and a good teammate takes those into account when putting their to-do list together. But sometimes, left to yourself, you might prioritize less productive tasks that still manage to keep you busy:

- Responding to every email that comes in as soon as it arrives

- Doing the tasks you enjoy more than those that might be higher priority

- Jumping to do whatever your manager asks, regardless of how important it is in the big picture

See the difference? These last things can keep us awfully busy, but the important work may not get done. How can we be smarter about how we prioritize our work?

When setting priorities, we need to think about how important this task is in both the short and long term. A lot of you are familiar with the concept of "important versus urgent." Urgent is the work that is time sensitive, pops up, and demands it be dealt with right away. But not all urgent work is important. That email might ask for an answer, but is answering it as important as finishing that report you're working on?

Important tasks are those that have long-term impact, maybe affecting other members of the team or the scope or results of a project. They require forward thinking and will have important results down the road, but there might not be an immediate win. But they don't always get our attention the way they should.

Remember being in school and your teacher assigning you a term paper a month before it was due? It was very important, but not very urgent. You had *plenty* of time. The night before it was due, it became urgent. Odds are you finished it, but it was more stressful (and possibly poorer quality) than it could and should have been.

Separating the urgent from the important isn't difficult when you take the time to breathe and look at the situation logically. There is something called the Pareto principle, sometimes known as the 80/20 rule. It says that 20 percent of the work you do garners you 80 percent of the results. Think about the opposite of that: over three-quarters of your tasks get you only a fifth of the results you need. When you look at a task, think about the impact for you and the team, and not just how quickly you can check it off your list.

Here are some of the things to consider when you start to get stressed about what work you should tackle first:

■ *Don't overbook yourself.* Stuff happens. When your task list is so full it doesn't allow room for things that pop up unexpectedly, you'll inevitably run into problems. Plan for a mix of small, easily accomplished tasks and larger blocks of time for meetings, project work, and catching up. And leave time open to provide the flexibility to respond to the unexpected.

■ *Share calendars with your team and be honest about your availability.* If you really need to focus for an hour, let your teammates know so you won't be interrupted or expected to respond right away. Most of us don't block anything except meetings on our calendars, and when people look at them, we seem to be available. Same with your status updates. This will help limit the number of urgent requests you have to respond to right away.

■ *Use your status updates on IM and email.* If you don't want to be disturbed for an hour, let your colleagues know. Just be sure to make yourself available again when you come up for air.

■ *Double-check your assumptions.* If you can't categorically state where a task falls on the priority list, don't be afraid to ask. Being proactive and asking your manager or your colleagues to give you guidance on setting priorities is hugely helpful. Wayne frequently asks Kevin, "You've given me three assignments over the last couple of days; which do you want me to do first?"

- *Consider the work styles of your teammates and customers.* Some people want details and lots of them. Others want only a quick and dirty answer so they can get on with their work. If you understand what your customer (whether they are internal or external) wants, you can put the appropriate energy in the right places and not spend time on unnecessary work. In chapter 7 we mentioned DISC as one way to figure out how to work with others. Just asking them is another.

An Old-School Approach to Making Requests

Remember that you get stressed and confused by the way some people hand work off to you—let's make sure we don't do the same thing to others! Here's an approach to sending and receiving messages that has been forgotten but is a great model for even the most modern communication tools.

Back in the day when secretaries answered the phone and had to pass messages on to others, the good ones had a five-step approach to making sure all the information was transmitted as accurately as possible. Here are the five steps to taking a phone message in the most productive way possible. You'll see how this applies to sending email:

1. *Who are you?* If you know the person, just greet them and move on. If this is your first contact, or you don't know the person well, take a moment to create context for the message: "Hi, this is Bob in Accounting, and here's why I'm reaching out to you." And remember to be polite just like mom taught you.

2. *When are you calling?* Emails are time stamped, but with voice mails this is critical information. Think of this as context for the reader. It is helpful to know when the request was made, even if the message is time stamped.

3. *What are you asking for?* The clearer the request, the easier it is for people to prioritize and comply.

4. *When do you need it?* Don't put people in a panic if they don't have to be.

5. *How would you like it?* The more specific you are, the less chance of misunderstanding, and the odds go up the job will be done right the first time.

Here's what this might look like in the real world: "Hi, Alice. I have a meeting coming up, and I need to report the latest customer satisfaction numbers. Can I please get them from you by Tuesday afternoon my time (keeping Alice's time zone in mind too), in an Excel file? If you can't, please let me know so I can make other arrangements."

If you do these five things with every message you send, regardless of the tool you use, it will be easy to work with you. In a perfect world you can help your colleagues respond to you in kind, meaning you'll be working together better than ever and building positive working connections.

Working with others is something we all do, and it's still hard. When you are working at a distance from each other, it is even harder, and potentially even more stressful. If you understand the work that needs to get done, use the tools and processes available in the right way, and prioritize your work effectively (while helping your teammates do the same), you are well on the way to working with others in the most productive way possible.

Pause and Reflect

▶ How well do you understand your own work and that of your teammates?

▶ Are there problems or frustrations you find with the team's work processes? If so, is that a symptom of a larger problem, or do you need to better understand those processes and their purposes?

▶ How comfortable are you that your to-do list reflects the correct priorities, not only for your work, but the team?

Chapter 13

Participating in Meetings

Joanna is like many remote workers. She knows that meetings, even virtual ones, provide a chance to connect with her leader and teammates and can support the work she does. But they are meetings! Too often they feel like an interruption to her and are boring. Besides that, they can be uncomfortable. When she has something she wants to say, she never knows when to say it, and often she feels ignored—an example of out of sight and out of mind.

Chances are, you know how Joanna feels—you've thought or felt some or all of what she's experienced. When it comes to working remotely and meetings, a remote teammate has four responsibilities:

1. Be prepared for the meeting.

2. Be present.

3. Be valuable.

4. Be diligent about follow-up.

Be Prepared

Have you ever logged into a conference call or online meeting and asked yourself, Why am I on this call? It's difficult to be engaged in a meeting when you don't know what it's about, or what your role is.

The first step to making sure that meetings don't waste your time is to know why you're there. Do you know the purpose of the meeting? Knowing that gives you a big leg up in being prepared. Knowing the purpose is the most important first step in your preparation for the meeting.

Purpose is often clarified by understanding the desired outcomes for the meeting. And different meetings have different desired outcomes.

Is the purpose of the meeting just to deliver information? If that's the case, your role is probably to be a sponge and suck that information up. Hopefully, there will be time for you to ask questions at the end, but your job is to do your best to focus, understand what's being delivered, take good notes, and decide for yourself what's next. That way you can act and make good use of everyone's time.

If the goal is to solve a problem or make a decision, you're going to be expected to contribute. After all, you're being paid to add value to the team. If the desired outcome is to build team cohesion and collaboration, you may be required to do some things that might not be your first instinct. That might include showering and being dressed in work-appropriate clothes, even when that's not something you do every day, so that you can use your webcam like everyone else.

If documents and meeting details are sent out in advance, it's your job to become familiar with the information, so rather than being a stumbling block, you help the meeting be successful.

A team member might show up on the call as requested, but that's just the start of their responsibility. "They told me to be here. I'm here"—isn't enough. Don't be that person! A great teammate shows up prepared and focused on helping the call or meeting achieve its objective.

But what if you don't know why you've been invited or the meeting's purpose? You need to be proactive and ask. You can ask a teammate what their understanding is. Often that's all you need to have your mind focused properly.

More importantly, you can ask your manager why you were invited and what you need to do to prepare for it. Position the question as a benefit to your boss and the team. If you ask, "Do I really have to attend?" it will sound whiny or self-serving. If you ask about the purpose of the meeting and how you can contribute, you are setting yourself up to serve and help everyone succeed.

When you ask the question effectively, nothing bad will happen, and one of three positive things will likely occur:

- You'll know your role in the meeting and what is expected of you. If your input is required, you'll be ready.

- You might find out you really need to be on the call as a compliance issue, or simply to get the same information at the same time as the rest of the team. At least you'll be able to give the meeting the attention it deserves.

- During the discussion it might become apparent that you don't need to be there at all. Often people call meetings and invite the same people out of habit. It's possible you can't really add value, suggesting you should bow out so you can work on other things on your list. More than that, with fewer people (assuming they are the right people) in the meeting, it will be easier to get results.

Once you know what the meeting is for and your expected role, your job is to be prepared to participate and contribute. If there is reading to be done, or they want you to come with questions or ideas, block the time you need to show up as an engaged, prepared meeting attendee.

Be Present

Being "present" on a meeting is more than simply having your name show up on the online participant list. It means giving the meeting your attention and best efforts.

When you're on the meeting, it's easy for your mind to drift. It's hard enough to stay focused, and when you're in the room, you at least have stuff and people to look at—and hopefully you are less likely to start answering your email. There's a social responsibility to at least pretend to pay attention that we don't have when we're online. And, of course, if you're on webcam, everyone can see you.

You can reduce and eliminate the possible distractions before the meeting begins by closing unnecessary apps and browser windows, and anything else that will just distract you, like pop-up notifications. Put your cell phone in a drawer so that you're not tempted to be on it or checking it. A great way to keep engaged is to make notes for yourself, especially if you know you'll be speaking and contributing to the topic at hand. By making notes, you keep both your brain and your body engaged.

By the way, when we say take notes, we're talking about good old pen and paper. First, your typing is likely distracting others and may lead them to think you aren't focused on the meeting. Also, studies show that connecting your hand, eyes, and brain increases your retention of the material and stimulates creative thinking.

Of course, you can stay really engaged by taking the "official" notes of the meeting. That way you will have to keep your mind on task, and since it's a job nobody else wants, your efforts will be appreciated.

The best way to stay focused is to be proactive. Offer to help. You can do things like be the timekeeper and keep an eye on the clock. You can take notes for the team (on the virtual whiteboard or on paper) so that everyone knows the next steps at the meeting's end.

Chances are you've been in what we call a "hybrid meeting"—where there is a group of people in a central location and others dialed in or connected through your meeting platform at a distance. We bet you've noticed some tensions that exist in that situation, including:

- The remote members can't hear because of the noise or many people talking at the same time in the conference room.

- The remote people can't get a comment into the conversation.

- The people in the conference seem to forget that other people are actually in the meeting!

Here are some solutions:

- If you are one of the people in the room or you're talking to the meeting leader beforehand, ask that there be a "speaker monitor," somebody whose job is to watch the speaker and make sure that papers aren't being rattled and things like that. And if people who are remote are trying to speak up, that person is deputized to say, "Wait a minute; Larry is trying to say something. Everybody please give him space. Go ahead, Larry." That will help.

- A "chat monitor" will also help give people who aren't speaking up a chance to participate.

- Ask that people manage the noise in the room, and if it's getting so loud that you can't hear, don't be afraid to let everyone know. People don't mean to be rude or exclude you, but they are thinking about who they can actually see. Again, this is something that you can talk to your manager or the meeting leader about. But one of the great frustrations of working remotely is the people in the room talk first and there's really nothing left to contribute. And yet if we don't contribute, they think we're not part of the team. This is a vicious cycle that serves no one.

- Ask that the meeting leader start the questions or comments with the people who are remote sometimes instead of just automatically going to the people in the room. And ask the people in the room to repeat and rephrase the information so that you're clear that you've heard it.

- Lose the conference room, sometimes. It may seem odd to have people who are in the same location all log in from their desk, but if it's the kind of meeting where everybody needs to be heard from and be involved, consider having everyone online using their webcams. This avoids most all the challenges we've discussed and levels the playing field and participation compared to the mixed meeting approach.

Remember these things don't happen intentionally, or because people don't care. Usually your manager and teammates are unaware of the problem. By professionally bringing it to their attention, everyone wins.

Be Valuable

Meetings may not be your favorite thing, but there is no better time to connect with all the members of your team and be a great teammate. You want to be both ethically visible and valuable.

Since you are going to attend the meeting, resolve to be a valuable part of it. There are many ways to do this, and they center on being both productive and proactive (two of the 3Ps).

Here's how you can help meeting productivity:

- *Be on time.* Most of us don't mean to be late; it's just hard to be on an eleven o'clock call if your ten o'clock meeting is still going on. There are a couple of ways to help this. One is to log into meetings early, even if you are still on another call, and stay on mute until you're available. Consider sending a quick chat message to the host explaining what's going on so people aren't waiting for you. The other way is to join the meeting as quietly as possible and not interrupt the proceedings. You can always IM with a colleague to catch up as long as it isn't a distraction and you're focusing on the meeting.

- *Be prepared.* We've already talked about how to do this.

- *Pay attention to the agenda.* The meeting was called to accomplish certain tasks. Don't be the person who derails the agenda. If you have a topic to discuss that wasn't planned (and before the meeting was the time to put it on the agenda—next time), ask if you can raise it and, if not, if it can be tabled for the next meeting. If your team doesn't always have an agenda, consider raising that idea as a process improvement. Agendas will almost always make virtual meetings more effective.

- *Follow up as needed.* If there are action items from the meeting or call, put them in your calendar or task list immediately so they don't slip your mind. Plan to complete them as required by the team.

Here's how your proactivity can help:

- *Volunteer to take a role.* The two most necessary (and often unassigned) tasks on a meeting are timekeeper and notetaker. Not only will you be visible to the team, you're saving someone else from doing it. Plus, if you want something done well . . . you know the rest.

- *Ask the question.* The detail that is nagging you is likely nagging others too—you aren't the only one wondering. Your teammates will appreciate your sparing them having to ask the question, and your boss will appreciate getting the information right the first time instead of having to hold another meeting or spending a lot of time with follow-up. And ask the question that no one wants to ask. Everyone knows that elephant is in the room (even if there is no physical room!). The team will benefit from getting the topic on the table.

■ *Use your chat tool.* Don't be shy about using chat or other ways to interact if providing input is difficult. You are on the meeting to add value.

Be Diligent about Follow-Up

One of the leading causes of bad meeting morale is that the previous meeting didn't accomplish what it should have and thus there's another meeting. Great teammates don't cause bad meetings.

When a meeting wraps up, there's a window of opportunity where follow-up will be either assured or pretty much guaranteed to fail—choose to be part of the solution:

■ Make sure everyone has a copy of the action items. Most meeting platforms allow you to make your own copy of the whiteboards and other documents. (If yours doesn't, ask for permission to do so; it's usually the click of a button.) Volunteer to send them out if needed.

■ Get those action items in your calendar. As soon as the meeting is over, block time for your assignments. You don't have to complete them right away (unless they're easy or the priority is high), but schedule time to do them so you don't forget.

■ Clarify with your manager or colleagues any questions you have about your action items. Better to look a little confused at first than spend time and energy and not give people what they need.

Final Thoughts

Meetings are a fact of organizational life—and perhaps they're more important to a team that works at a distance. When you use the ideas in this chapter, you will help the team accomplish more in meetings. Done well, meetings also provide you a way to be ethically visible and build stronger working relationships.

Pause and Reflect

▶ How active have you been as a participant in meetings?

▶ What could you do to support better meetings and outcomes?

Part 3

You and Your Future

Being a great teammate is about how you work with the rest of your team, your manager, and your organization to satisfy your customers. That means that you are focused on others—whether your teammates, the organization, or your customers. That is wonderful—and remember that you can be externally focused and engaged *and* still get what you need from your working experience. Thinking about your needs doesn't make you selfish. Ask yourself these questions:

- Why do you work?

- Why do you have the job you currently hold?

- Where do you want to be in a year? Or five years?

If you're honest, the answers are intensely personal. You work to keep a roof over your head. You have to support your family and maintain and hopefully improve your lifestyle. And, if you are at the beginning of your career, the answers will likely be very different than if you are at the end of your working life.

Whatever the question, the answer ultimately is about you. We are all driven by what's important to us as individuals. Why do we work hard and focus on productivity? Some of it is enjoying and being challenged by the work, but if we don't meet or surpass standards, we won't be employed very long. If it's not interesting, or we think it is dull and won't get any better, we might keep plugging away, but we won't be as engaged, productive, or proactive and won't be thinking about the long-term potential for our careers and lives.

Why do you take on that extra work or volunteer for that project? It's important to the team, but you're probably interested in it. And maybe you just love a challenge. There might be a promotion or a bonus in it for you.

If you're a contractor, you know that finding satisfying work with good people isn't easy, so you want to make sure you maintain the relationships that enable you to find work you enjoy and keep the contracts coming. If you don't enjoy this particular engagement, you might be looking for another opportunity while working on this one. While there is nothing wrong with that, it's still in your best interest to give 100 percent to this less-than-awesome engagement even if you have your eyes open.

In the following chapters, you'll read a lot about taking care of yourself and planning for your future in a mindful, ethically responsible way. You might feel uncomfortable thinking this way (especially if your employer paid for the book!), but let's ask some final questions:

Who cares about your work as much as you do? Who is most invested in your future?

Focusing solely on today while ignoring the future is a big reason people quit reaching out, building connections, learning new skills, or caring about their tasks, teammates, and ultimately, jobs.

As you read further, remember:

- It's okay to look at your work now and think about the future.

- It's okay to balance your work and your personal life in a way that works for you and your family.

- It's okay to plan now for the next step of your working life, whatever that is.

    In fact, if you don't, who will?

Chapter 14

Taking Care of Yourself

Al has been working from home for a while now and mostly enjoys it. He gets more time with the family, and the work is rewarding. He's noticed, though, that he doesn't have much time to himself. He used to read on the train into the office, and often sang along with the radio in the car. Now he either is working or has someone else with him all the time. He eats at his desk and can't remember the last time he had lunch or an after-work beverage with a coworker. And why don't his pants fit?

Being a great teammate sounds like a selfless act; we help our managers, we look out for and coach our teammates, and everything is for our customers. What about us?

Yes, there are many positives to working from home. Being alone also means being alone with your thoughts (which aren't always positive or productive) and often being lonely, indulging in poor habits, and working in ways that aren't physically good for you.

And while we want you to be at your best for your own reasons, if you're not healthy, motivated, engaged, and relatively sane, it's difficult to be productive, be proactive, or think about the potential of your work.

We believe there are two big areas you need to consider when thinking about self-care:

- Your physical comfort and well-being

- Work and home life balance

Your Physical Comfort and Well-Being

Taking care of yourself physically when you're working alone sounds easy. You have more control than when you are at the office, and it's not like you don't know what to do, right? But let's ask that question another way: Under the best of conditions, do you get enough sleep and exercise? Are you eating right and working in a way that's good for your body?

Imagine you are worried about your job security, trying to take care of your teammates, and striving for a promotion and you already know you should be better about your eating habits, sleep, and exercise. Are you suddenly going to be a health nut and do everything right?

Here are some things you can do to make working remotely better for you physically:

- *Get enough sleep.* More than a third of American adults are not getting enough sleep on a regular basis, according to a study in the Morbidity and Mortality Weekly Report from the Centers for Disease Control and Prevention (CDC). You would think that because remote workers don't have to fight traffic or catch a train, it would be easier to get some z's. It's not.

  When working remotely, you may feel like you are at the beck and call of the telephone, email, instant messages, and the like. Because we carry our devices with us all the time, it's almost impossible to ignore the onslaught of information, questions, and tasks. So much so that some people check emails if they get up in the middle of the night or before they're even out of bed. Here are some guidelines that can help:

  - *Stop checking your phone a half hour before bedtime.* The blue-spectrum light of a digital screen actually interferes with our brain's sleep patterns. Set it to charge somewhere out of arm's reach so you won't be as tempted to check it when you should be thinking about sleep.

  - *Get an old-school alarm clock.* Many people now use their phone as their alarm clock, but checking to see what time it is has the same impact as checking your email. People slept, knew what time it was, and got up with the alarm long before the iPhone.

▸ *Set a natural rhythm.* Find a bedtime and waking-up time that work for your body, and stick to that schedule as much as possible. You can always DVR or watch your favorite late-night show online later. It might feel awkward and unnatural at first, but creating a healthier sleep pattern will become your new norm. Your body and mind will thank you.

▸ *Limit caffeine, alcohol, and sugars before bed.* Our body's chemistry is delicate, and most of us are highly susceptible to these chemical stimulants. Check to make sure what you drink or eat doesn't contain these ingredients in sneaky amounts. If you're a bit older, you shouldn't drink fluids ninety minutes before bed anyway, or you'll be waking up in the middle of the night.

▸ *Take a nap.* Your body is trying to tell you something. Don't tell Kevin, but because Wayne is on the West Coast and often starts work before six a.m., he's been known to take a twenty-minute siesta in the early afternoon just because it's better for him than a cup of coffee that will keep him awake later. Try not to nap too late in the afternoon, though, or you won't be tired at bedtime.

■ *Engage in physical activity.* Not everyone is a gym bunny with an athletic club membership and a physical trainer on speed dial. But whether you have a normal exercise routine or not, sitting staring at a screen for hours at a time, or hunched over your work, is bad for you in so many ways. We're not going to nag you about any of that, but no matter what your normal level of fitness or activity, or even if you have a physical disability, some things need to happen.

■ *Schedule breaks.* When we're caught up in a flurry of work, or on deadline, or just feeling like everyone else is working so we should be too, we often spend too much time at our work space. Take time every hour or so (set an alarm if you must) to get up, stretch, and give your eyes a momentary break. One great tip is to take those household chores that are gnawing at you while you're working and make them your excuse. Going downstairs to throw a load of laundry in is still pausing, bending, walking, and not staring into a screen. If you have flexibility, build time for a walk or a run or just doing some stretches. You don't have to name the time on your calendar; just mark yourself as busy and stretch those quads.

- *Get outside.* Always remember that fresh air, even for a few minutes at a time, is better than staying inside breathing the same recycled atmosphere.

- *Find physical activity that works for you.* Maybe you aren't cut out to bench press two hundred pounds or do an hour on the elliptical machine. Walking the dog or playing tag with your kid for a few minutes will still give you the mental and physical break you need. Take the stairs instead of the elevator. Ride a bike to the corner store.

- *Eat healthy.* You'd think that because you're in your own home, and you do the shopping, you'd be able to easily indulge in healthy eating. But if you weren't speed eating quinoa on a regular basis before, you won't suddenly start just because you're working from home. Many people find that stress, loneliness, or boredom often cause them to eat more junk food than ever. Plan your meals, especially breakfast, with an eye to high protein, low sugar foods, and keep healthy snacks within reach so you won't go for the chips or candy. Nuts, dried fruit, and even low-fat/low-salt microwave popcorn are good alternatives to the more tempting junk food. Find something you like and substitute it for your old standbys.

- *Work in a way that is good for your body.* Most of us, when we worked in the office, had a proper desk or work space, and a good office chair. Now that you're working from home, you might be working from the kitchen table or move to the sofa. We had big, beautiful monitors on our old desk, but now we're squinting at a laptop and using the touch pad instead of a mouse. These less-than-ideal work conditions can cause chronic pain (especially in the back and neck), headaches, and weight gain. If your company pays for your office equipment, take advantage of the situation. If they don't, and your organization or your budget won't provide for new equipment, you can find good chairs in thrift shops and used but functional monitors online.

Remember, we aren't doctors or nutritionists. If you need professional information, talk to your health professionals, or check out the resources of the

Mayo Clinic—who have wonderful, easy-to-follow guidelines for work-from-home ergonomics.[1]

Work and Home Life Balance

When you worked in an office and thought about work-life balance, it usually meant you were missing family or social activities because of work. But what if Daddy is at home but still missing dinner because he's on a conference call—again? Are you missing snuggle time with the little ones because you have to be on that Zoom call to India? These are work-life balance issues too.

- *Balance isn't some arbitrary formula or perfect destination.* Work in the real world doesn't fit neatly into the traditional nine-to-five, and family and personal commitments change constantly. Don't get fooled into thinking work-life balance is some magical formula. It's what works so that you are meeting your commitments to your employer, yourself, and those close to you. It won't be the same as everyone else, and what it means will change throughout your career. If you work in an accounting firm, you know that tax time will be crazy and you'll spend more time at work. Are you reclaiming that time somewhere else when things ease up, or is it gone forever?

- *Build physical distance between your work and personal space.* If you are lucky enough to have a separate work room or home office, make sure that your hobby doesn't also take place in that same space. If you work out of your bedroom, make sure that when you are not working, the laptop is closed and the monitor shut down so that you will be less likely to dive back into work. If you work from the dining room table and need to leave things out for the next day, put a sheet over everything. The visual cues will help you more than you realize.

- *Have something that gives you pleasure, and schedule time for it.* You cannot work, or think about work, or talk about work, all the time without it bleeding over into your personal time and relationships. It's important that you have things outside of your job that bring you pleasure, and indulge in them.

Kevin collects antique John Deere tractors and goes to auctions. (Really, it's a thing.) Wayne writes novels and attends a local writing group when he's not teaching people how to lead virtual meetings. We both have families we enjoy spending time with. We work long hours, and love it, but it is absolutely true that all work and no play makes Jack, or Jacqueline, a very dull person. It also burns them out and can lead to depression or disengagement.

■ *Share your passions and outside interests with your teammates and your manager.* Do you know what your teammates care about? It gives you something to talk about other than tasks and numbers, and often helps build personal relationships and connections. Does your boss know you have a thing for butterflies? It won't come as much of a surprise, then, when you ask for a day off to attend the lepidopterist conference in your town, and they may even encourage you to take the extra day. Balancing your work and home life doesn't mean you can't acknowledge both.

■ *Spend some time on your own spiritual, mental, and social development.* We talk a lot about your responsibilities to your teammates and your family, but what about you? What are you doing to help center your own being? This isn't some new-age question. It's vital to people that we learn new things and challenge ourselves, and we're not talking about work. We'll discuss professional development in the next chapter.

Taking time to read, start a hobby, meditate, or just do something that makes you happy is not a selfish act, unless it means you're ignoring your other duties. Choose a nonwork-related book and schedule time for a chapter or two a night. Get to that religious service you've been skipping, learn to meditate, or take up the harmonica (hey, you could even practice the harmonica on your break—buying a tractor, not so much).

If it makes you happy and gives you more energy, the people around you will notice. Both your family and teammates will see the difference in you for all the best reasons. You will have the energy and mental bandwidth to sustain your work and personal lives and enjoy life more.

Many people put others ahead of themselves, and likely will continue to do so regardless of where they work. But getting some measure of control and pleasure that eases our stress, makes us happy, and eliminates the physical miseries of modern life makes it not just important, but mandatory.

Allow yourself to treat yourself as well as you treat others.

Pause and Reflect

▶ What actions do you take to make sure you are healthy physically, mentally, and emotionally?

▶ What do you know is important that you don't do (often enough)?

Chapter 15

Planning Your Career Path

Jim loves being part of a virtual team and thinks he might make a good project manager. When he was in the office, he began taking little assignments that demonstrated his manager had faith in him, but since he's started working from home, he hasn't been assigned any extra tasks or asked if he wants to take the lead on team work. He wonders what is going on, and what he should do about it.

Unless you are two weeks from retirement, you have a long work life ahead of you. How you spend it is up to you.

We are all thinking about the future. If you're ambitious at all, you're probably thinking of this job as the current step in a long process of moving to ever more challenging and rewarding positions. If you're a contractor or gig worker, even if you like your current arrangement, you always must be thinking about what's next. Regardless of your situation, one thing is true: nobody cares as much about your career and development as you do.

Thinking about the future is an important part of staying engaged and motivated. If you can't imagine the next day being better than this one, or getting you closer to a personal goal, why work so hard? In the end, today's work, while important, isn't enough to sustain and propel you forward.

We don't mean you should spend all your time thinking about the future. Those reports need to be done now, and Amy in Payables needs that information—both need to be done, and neither will likely impact whether you become CEO one day.

How is this different when you work remotely? Just as your manager and teammates are "out of sight, out of mind" to you, you may not be on the radar screen of those who do the hiring and promoting. Sometimes organizations believe that if you work from home, you have decided work-life balance is more important than your career track. When you work apart from everyone else, you might proactively be networking to make the connections that could further your career. It's up to you to keep yourself informed and moving forward.

You should spend some time thinking about more than this week's task list. When you have (or hopefully make) a few moments, consider:

- What do you want for your professional/work life in a year, in five years, and before you retire?

- What opportunities exist with your current employer?

- What is going on in your industry or field of interest, and what part would you like to play?

In this chapter, we want you thinking about where you want to be, and how you spot opportunities to move forward.

Are you single or planning a family? Does living where you are matter to you, or are you willing to pack up and move? Do you see yourself as an individual contributor with no interest in leading others, or are you on a management track? Which do you prefer: staying in your current industry or performing the same role in a different kind of company?

What Do You Want from Your Professional Life?

We bet if we asked this question six months ago the answer might be different than it is today, and it will definitely not be the same a year from now. That is why it's important that you take time once in a while to see where you're headed, and if you like the trajectory your working life is taking.

- *Consider both the short and long term.* You probably won't be the VP of Sales tomorrow, but that doesn't mean staying where you are indefinitely. Maybe you want to move to handling national accounts, or you think being a team leader is more your style. If you are considering a full-time project management role, what smaller tasks or assignments can you take on that will get you there?

Is the work you have in front of you moving you toward that goal? If not, give some thought to what the next steps might be.

- *Find out what your manager or organization has planned for you.* You might work for a company that does yearly goal setting and performance plans, or has a succession planning program. If so, that's a great place to start, but it's not enough. Remember, when the company creates a plan for you, that's their vision for the company or the team, and how they believe you fit in. It may or may not match your vision for the future. Most of us don't have honest discussions with our managers or people inside the company about what we want. If you see yourself in a certain position, share that vision with your manager and others inside the organization.

As a remote worker, you need to find out one very important thing. Will being remote impact your chances for a desirable transfer or promotion? Some companies assume that if you choose to work from home you've chosen lifestyle over interest in the company. Other times you just aren't on the hiring manager's radar because they don't see you in the office all the time. If relocating or going back to a commute is the tradeoff for getting that next position, you need to decide if that's right for you. If it isn't, then what?

Most people are happy to just plod along, waiting for the next raise or a promotion to appear in the "natural" order of things. Not everyone is likely as ambitious or proactive as you are. Make sure your leader knows your goals and desires. Good leaders recognize the importance of helping people achieve their goals. When you share your goals with your leader, they will be more likely to coach and support you. That's part of their job, and you being proactive will help them do it.

What Opportunities Exist in Your Current Company?

Looking to advance in your career is more than simply waiting for your manager to get promoted or quit so you can get their job. If you work for a large organization, there may be opportunities in other departments or disciplines that can use your skills. In fact, traditional corporations often require that people work cross-division if they want to advance so they have a bigger picture of how things work.

One of the joys of working remotely is that you are away from the gossip and talk about things that you don't care about and don't impact your work directly. But not all water-cooler talk is useless gossip. Just as we sometimes ignore the rest of our teammates in the interest of getting our own work done, we sometimes shut out news from the rest of our organization because it doesn't immediately impact us.

But what about your future? Some things to consider:

- *How well do you understand what's going on in your company?* Are you reading the newsletters and announcements, or do you think that news doesn't concern you and delete them? We know that if we stopped what we were doing and read every email, it would get in the way of work and often waste our time. Create an email folder just for company news, and then once a week or so take a few minutes to read through it for useful information, job postings, and the like.

- *How well do you know the people in your organization outside your own teammates?* When you correspond with others in your company, do you take the time to build relationships with them like you do your own teammates? When you're thinking about future opportunities, this matters a lot. According to LinkedIn, over half of all job postings are filled by internal referrals.[1] When people get promoted, try sending a simple congratulatory email. Take a moment to engage them on more than a transactional basis.

- *How well do you know the ins and outs of finding opportunities in your organization?* Some companies post job openings and opportunities on their intranet. Some announce them in newsletters, and some positions are filled before the rest of the world even hears about them. While you don't want to spend too much time obsessing about this, making sure you are in the loop can mean you have a better opportunity to hear about those openings earlier. You need to be proactive.

What's Going On in Your Industry or Field of Interest?

Even if you enjoy where you work now and want to progress within the organization, you will have a clearer picture of where you're going (and be seen as more valuable to the organization) if you understand what's going on in the world beyond your team.

You can be a better teammate by offering outside perspective and knowing what the competition is up to. Understanding industry trends can add value to team discussions. It will also point the way to new skills you might need or knowledge you'll have to gain in order to stay employable.

- *Network outside your organization.* The simplest tool to start with is LinkedIn. Find groups in your industry or read articles that intrigue you. Connect with people who write interesting posts, or simply lurk and learn from others who are interested in the same things you are. Just know that the more active you are commenting, "liking," and offering to connect, the more you'll come to know. You may also find people in your own company you haven't met yet who share your passions.

- *Read trade journals and newsletters.* Almost every industry has hundreds of online journals and newsletters available. Subscribing to them all will make you crazy and bury you, but choosing a few really great resources will open a whole new world to you. Add them but be sure to go through periodically and unsubscribe from what doesn't give you what you need.

- *Join an association.* There are over six thousand associations in the United States. Most are grouped by industry or specialty. Membership, or even associate membership where you have access to their learning materials, is a great way to see what's going on in the world outside your team. Your manager may even have budget to help you pay for membership dues or events. Know that with such groups, you usually get out of them what you put in, so be an active member, not just a lurker. Just like engaging at work is to your advantage, the same is true with industry and professional associations.

Nobody cares about your professional development as much as you do. Take stock of your future and be mindful about your next steps. Don't leave your future up to other people.

Pause and Reflect

▶ When was the last time you thought about your long-term career goals?

▶ Have you shared those goals with your manager or others who might be able to help? If not, why not?

Chapter 16

Managing Your Learning and Growth

Toni doesn't miss her commute—except that on the train she could read or listen to podcasts, and in the car she always had an audiobook playing. When she started to work from home, she didn't realize she'd miss that part of the commute. That time seems now to be lost. She just isn't getting as much reading done as she used to do. More than that, she always enjoyed the training sessions her company ran, but lately she has not been getting asked to participate, or even been hearing about them until it's too late. She feels like she's stagnating a bit.

You are responsible for your own career development and upgrading your skills. That's true whether you work in an office or from home, miles away from world headquarters. What is unique about working remotely is you may have more control and responsibility for making it happen whether it's part of your "individual development plan" or not. We can't say this enough: it's not that your manager and your organization don't care about you and your career goals. They just don't care as much as you do (or should).

In your current work environment, you have more flexibility in your schedule. When there is a learning opportunity like a webinar, you likely can either block out time on your calendar to watch it live or view the recording without someone stopping by your desk every ten minutes to interrupt or judge you.

But many of us have relied on the structure of the workplace and the organization to help us grow our skills. HR sends out notifications about upcoming classes. Your manager works with you on that individual development plan. You know, that plan that is created each year with the expectation that you will follow through, but often falls by the wayside. Even with the best of intentions, neither you nor your boss pays enough attention to it because you're too busy doing the "real work." You hear from coworkers about this class or that cool article that was so informative and helpful, but you aren't around to take advantage of it.

You want to grow your skills and become more productive. That requires being proactive and thinking about the potential impact on your work and goals. Learning, developing skills, and growing as a worker and as a human being is how you make the 3P Model a real, living part of your professional life.

While "you can learn something new every day" is true, learning and developing new capabilities takes focus, planning, and effort. Done right, it will be rewarding and fun.

Self-directed learning can take many forms:

- Traditional training and learning available through your organization or elsewhere

- Investing in yourself

- Reading books, magazines, and online articles

- Listening to podcasts and other free resources

An underappreciated way to learn is to stop and reflect on your work experiences, interactions, and results. You can learn from both what worked and what didn't.

Traditional Training and Learning through Your Organization

Most organizations have training available in many different forms: traditional classrooms, virtual sessions, e-learning, and more. Here are some ways you might want to take advantage of what's available to you:

- *Talk to your manager and people in your organization about your goals.* If you've been having conversations about your goals with your boss or people in the organization such as HR and training, make sure you also ask, "What should I be learning now?"

Sometimes people will be able to recommend a course of action or next steps. Often, though, you'll have to do your own research. Go into the training or HR portals on your intranet or learning management system, and search for classes or learning opportunities. Remember to talk to your teammates as well, especially those who have the skills you desire.

- *Go directly to the people in your organization to talk about funding.* Your manager may or may not have a discretionary budget for training, but HR or Learning and Development may have other ways to pay for, or reimburse you for, your development, even outside your own company. The answer might be no, but it won't hurt to ask.

- *Bookmark the learning calendars and schedules in your organization.* Check in periodically (monthly maybe?). See what's been added or scheduled so you can be proactive.

- *Talk to others in the organization and ask what they're learning.* Because individual development plans are personal, your teammates may know about opportunities that haven't been brought expressly to you. Ask what they're doing, and if they took a course or a program, find out if it was worth the investment. Maybe even pick their brain for the high points.

- *Invest your time.* Schedule and block time for your development.

Investing in Yourself

Just because the organization doesn't have the right course or program or the budget for you doesn't mean that needs to stop you.

From getting a college degree to being certified as an Agile guru to figuring out how to manage your time, a lot of what you'll want to learn is for your personal benefit. It's possible (but don't assume!) the organization won't make the investment for you. Here are some tips for getting the most from your investment and making it worthwhile. And don't forget to ask about reimbursement for courses you take; sometimes there's money available to get some or all of your investment back.

■ *Break the elephant into bite-sized chunks.* Even if you want a degree, you get there one course at a time. While it might be nice to take a whole series of interrelated classes on Excel, start with the introduction, or cherry-pick the specific modules that will most interest or benefit you.

■ *Seek less expensive alternatives.* There is no shortage of content outside your company, from a Harvard MBA to free webinars. While to some extent you get what you pay for, take advantage of low-cost and even free training to begin with. Udemy and LinkedIn Learning are just a couple of places to start. E-learning is often inexpensive and can be targeted to a specific need.

   If you belong to a professional association, one of the most important benefits is free or low-cost education. Depending on what you do, some companies pay for these memberships.

Reading Books, Magazines, and Online Articles

Reading is one of the best self-development habits you can develop. Think about areas you want to learn about and develop your skills in and then dive in.

■ *Books.* We are preaching to the choir here. If you are still reading, you understand the value books can bring to you. Don't stop now. Find new books by asking your teammates, leaders, or others you respect. Used books are inexpensive, and libraries are free.

■ *Magazine subscriptions.* This may seem old school, but magazines (and now online subscriptions) allow you to consume bite-sized chunks of content on your own schedule.

■ *Blogs, LinkedIn articles, and white papers.* The amount of quality content available to you to help you develop any specific part of your skillset is astounding. And the price is definitely right.

■ *Book clubs.* A great way to gain value from a book is to talk about it with others. As you are becoming more proactive and engaged, perhaps a book club with your teammates could serve several useful purposes.

Podcasts and Other Free Resources

The internet gives us access to most of the collected knowledge of the world, and yet humans spend most of their online time screaming at strangers on social media and watching cat videos. There's a ton of available information if you curate and consume it thoughtfully:

- *Podcasts.* Sure, podcasts can be a pleasant way to be entertained, but there are many podcasts that offer you access to the brightest minds on the planet. Choose carefully, and you will benefit greatly.

- *Free webinars.* The world is full of free webinars and videos on almost every topic, but as people who offer webinars and YouTube videos regularly, we need to give you this warning: a free webinar is (or should be) a learning opportunity, but it is often *not* training. And there is no such thing as a free lunch—don't be annoyed when the content or the person leading the session tries to sell you something. It's the reason you got this opportunity for free. Usually it is okay to register even if you can't join at the prescribed time—just make sure that your registration includes access to the recording later.

- *Newsletters and free downloads.* A lot of the world's leading experts (and people you've never heard of who know their stuff) offer daily, weekly, or monthly information in exchange for getting you on their mailing list. A lot of this is worth reading; it is free and comes right to you. It can also be a lot to manage. (Some of ours are listed at the end of the chapter.)

  Here are some ways to manage the onslaught. First, remember that if you can subscribe, you can also unsubscribe, usually with one click. If you want a free e-book or article, you can sign up and get what you need, then unsubscribe. Second, start a separate email folder for this kind of information. Set up a filter in your Outlook or Gmail to send these announcements to a folder so it doesn't clutter your in-box. Some people even create a separate email address to manage their learning resources all in one place. Do whatever allows you to focus on work when you need to—but have access to these great resources so you can read them at your leisure.

■ *Pick the brains of your teammates.* The best free resources are the very bright people you work with. A high-performing team is a learning team. You can gather only so much information by yourself, but if you read an article, someone else sits in on a webinar and gets the visuals, a third person reads a book, and each of you shares that information, you've tripled your knowledge in no time.

You can share this information informally in conversation with your teammates ("Hey, read anything good this week?"). More effective is to create a place to share articles, links to great information, and files you've downloaded. This can be on your shared drive, or in tools like Microsoft Teams and Slack. Just as you can create a "water cooler" channel for personal information, creating a "library" or "learning center" channel can help everyone get smarter.

You can also encourage the sharing of information during meetings. Kevin has a "what did you learn" section in his meetings and sometimes assigns book reports. (It's not as bad as it sounds.) Talk to your manager and teammates about what would work best in your environment.

Working remotely can overwhelm you and make it difficult to take time for your own learning. It also provides opportunities the likes of which we've never seen. Whether you want to learn basic coding or Zen meditation, the world is open to you, if you choose to embrace it.

Finally, document as much of your learning as you can. Especially if you attend webinars or take online classes, get proof of completion or certificates. Keep them in an electronic file, or print and save them, and add them to your LinkedIn profile so you can prove you've been developing your potential. It looks good at performance review time and can make the personal development discussion much easier. It also helps when applying for positions within the company to demonstrate how seriously you take your personal and career growth.

Pause and Reflect

► What are the skills and knowledge that will benefit your professional growth? What about your personal interests?

► How can you find these opportunities in your organization?

► What opportunities are there for low-cost or free learning elsewhere?

Online Resource

To subscribe to our weekly newsletter, *Unleashing Your Remarkable Potential,* go to:

KevinEikenberry.com/uyrp

Part 4

If You Lead Others

Chapter 17

Leading Great Remote Teammates

Melissa is leading her remote team, and she is now remote too. It is a different world for her—more so than she expected. She wants to be an effective leader, but she is dealing with all the challenges of being remote and trying to be the leader too. The fact that her VP is at headquarters doesn't make it easier.

This book is for team members, and we've already written a book for remote leaders. Yet, many people are in Melissa's boat. They aren't just leading remote teams; they work remotely themselves. This chapter is especially for you.

The Leader's Three Hats

Every leader wears at least three hats, even if they don't think about it, even if some of the hats are gathering dust in the closet:

- *The leader hat.* Yes, you are the leader of the team.

- *The team member hat.* Every leader is a member of at least two teams—the team of your peers, and the team you lead. As the leader, you're still a member of the team.

- *The communicator hat.* Every leader is a communication conduit from their team upward, and from more senior leadership downward. You need to be the face and voice of the team passing information up, and the face and voice of senior management communicating downward.

This chapter is included to help leaders when they wear each of these hats.

As the Leader of a Remote Team

If you have read this book because you want to help your remote team members "engage and connect," we salute you. We bet (especially if you didn't just skip to this chapter) that you are already doing many things right as a leader. We humbly suggest you also read our book *The Long-Distance Leader: Rules for Remarkable Remote Leadership* if you haven't yet. Here are some lessons we hope you take from this book and apply as you lead your team.

You may have noticed several topics that would more traditionally be in a leadership book than a team member book, including things like clear expectations and giving and receiving feedback. That is on purpose. These aren't skills that should be reserved for leaders, not as we view an engaged and highly productive workforce.

If you have team members reading this book, they are going to raise the bar on what they expect of you. If you have read the book, hopefully you will raise the bar for yourself and the team, too. "Engaged and connected" is a higher bar than "opening your laptop and doing the tasks you've been given." The good news is that when you raise those expectations and support people, you will see them flourish.

We believe in the potential of people. When you give them opportunities to step up, especially when they are working remotely, they will. Give them more tangible and meaningful ways to contribute and they will thrill you with their results.

If your team hasn't read this book yet, use it as a blueprint for your team development. Create a book club around the book, and let the team lead it. Each chapter will fuel conversations, build relationships, and give your team a collective picture of how they can work together better. Once you let them see what is possible for themselves and each other, let them engage and contribute in new ways. This will jumpstart the engagement of your remote team in valuable ways.

As a Remote Team Member

If you are working remotely yourself, this book isn't just for your team—it's for you. If you have been reading it thinking about how this would help your team in general, or with a specific challenge, you have gotten only a fraction of the value from these pages. You aren't just leading remote work, you are working remotely! As a remote worker, this book is for *you*, not just "your team."

If you want them to improve their productivity, their routines, their relationship building, and all the rest, what about you?

How would your team grade you as a teammate?

And what about the team of your peers? How are you doing in your relationships and trust building with them? How effective are those virtual meetings?

As the Communication Conduit

Organizational communication is hard, regardless of where people work. It's harder when people are at a distance. This means you must take your role as a communication conduit from your team upward and from management downward more seriously, and work at it harder.

Make sure you know what is going on with your team, not just with the work, but also with their emotions and stress. How are they feeling about the latest corporate initiative? Do you know how it affects them every day? Do you understand the unintended consequences of those decisions or new assignments so you can help to mitigate them?

If you don't know where your team is, you can't be their face and voice upward.

Hone your communication skills and tool usage for sharing organizational messages too. Forwarding the email or sending a quick follow-up email asking for questions likely isn't enough. Do you understand those messages well enough yourself? Are you taking the time to intentionally decide how to share them with your team? Are you considering richness versus scope (see "Picking the Right Tool" in chapter 7) when thinking about processes and which tools to use under what conditions? Are you having individual and team conversations to ensure understanding of organizational communication and direction?

The tools in this book will help you do both parts of this job better when you use them.

The Larger Organizational View

If you are a more senior leader or if you have been reading this book and thinking about how to support your remote teams and team members, there are a few things for you to think about too. Here is your to-do list (you are welcome):

- *Do your systems support the health of your remote teams?* Are you rewarding the right behaviors and providing the specific types of training they need?

- *Are you thinking about your remote workers?* Do they have the chance to work on bigger, more meaningful (and perhaps cross-functional) projects and teams? Are they appropriately considered for promotions, or are they in the "they want to work remotely" bucket, and automatically or unintentionally passed over?

- *Do all your processes work for people who are working away from the office?* Maybe for you this is still a small part of your employee population, but that number will likely grow. Are you taking care of them in the ways that are needed?

   If you think about moving to remote work or remaining with remote work as a cost-saving measure or an employee perk, please stop. While those may both be benefits that accrue from people working remotely, you must think about this approach as a valid and effective way for work to happen and people/teams to thrive, not as a tactic.

   We are writing these words in September 2020 during a pandemic that is changing how people view work and are reexamining a lot of long-held assumptions. We don't know when or how quickly work will return to "normal." But we bet that the trend toward remote work, even if it is just some of the time, is going to continue. If your culture has always been that people come to a central location every day, you might need to rethink that approach. This book gives you a road map for making remote work successful. We hope it helps you and your teams.

Pause and Reflect

▶ As a remote worker, what are the challenges you experience that your team might be dealing with as well?

▶ As a leader, are you doing your job as a conduit for information from the organization to the team, and vice versa? What can you do better?

▶ What policies are in place that may make remote work more difficult or unappealing to people over the long haul? What are they, and what should they be?

Final Thoughts

The world of work has changed and is changing constantly. Working remotely using technology is part of that change. There is much you know from your work and life experience about relating to, communicating with, and working with others. But it is different once separated by distance, culture, nationalities, and perhaps multiple time zones.

We hope this book helps everyone who is working in a home office, at their kitchen table, or from a coffee shop be more productive and successful. But we hope for more than that.

We want this book to help you achieve what the subtitle promises—help people engage and connect. When you do this, everyone wins. At an individual level, work becomes more meaningful and purposeful. As a team you will be more successful and perhaps have some fun. The organization and the people they serve win too.

Ultimately that is our goal with this book—to help people see the ways that they can be engaged with each other and the work and feel connected socially and emotionally even if they are distanced physically.

If we can help you or your organization expand or implement these ideas, please let us know.

Notes

Part 1 introduction

1 BusinessDictionary, s.v. "team," accessed June 9, 2020, http://www
.businessdictionary.com/definition/team.html.

Chapter 1

1 *Merriam-Webster*, s.v. "proactive," accessed June 20, 2020, https://www
.merriam-webster.com/dictionary/proactive.

Chapter 4

1 Nicholas Bloom, "To Raise Productivity, Let More Employees Work from
Home," *Harvard Business Review*, January/February 2014, https://hbr.org
/2014/01/to-raise-productivity-let-more-employees-work-from-home.

2 David M. Sanbonmatsu, "Who Multi-Tasks and Why? Multi-Tasking Ability, Perceived Multi-Tasking Ability, Impulsivity, and Sensation Seeking,"
PLOS ONE, January 23, 2013.

3 John Brandon, "The Surprising Reason Millennials Check Their Phones
150 Times a Day," Inc.com, April 17, 2017, https://www.inc.com/john
-brandon/science-says-this-is-the-reason-millennials-check-their-phones
-150-times-per-day.html.

Chapter 5

1 *Cambridge English Dictionary*, s.v. "routine," accessed June 20, 2020,
https://dictionary.cambridge.org/us/dictionary/english/routine.

Chapter 6

1 Brené Brown, "Clear Is Kind. Unclear Is Unkind," *Brené Brown* (blog), October 15, 2018, https://brenebrown.com/blog/2018/10/15/clear-is -kind-unclear-is-unkind/.

Chapter 7

1 Bettina Büchel, *Using Communication Technology* (New York: Palgrave, 2001).

Chapter 9

1 "Research on Friends at Work," Olivet Nazarene University, accessed June 20, 2020, https://online.olivet.edu/news/research-friends-work.

2 Jessica R. Methot et al., "Are Workplace Friendships a Mixed Blessing? Exploring Tradeoffs of Multiplex Relationships and Their Associations with Job Performance," Wiley Online Library, April 8, 2015, https://onlinelibrary .wiley.com/doi/full/10.1111/peps.12109.

Chapter 11

1 Dictionary.com, s.v. "feedback," accessed June 20, 2020, https://www .dictionary.com/browse/feedback.

Chapter 14

1 "Office Ergonomics: Your How-To Guide," Mayo Clinic (website), April 27, 2019, https://www.mayoclinic.org/healthy-lifestyle/adult-health/in-depth /office-ergonomics/art-20046169.

Chapter 15

1 *Global Talent Trends 2020: 4 Trends Changing the Way You Hire and Retain Talent*, LinkedIn, January 22, 2020, https://business.linkedin.com/talent -solutions/resources/talent-strategy/global-talent-trends-2020-report.

Acknowledgments

We will be forever thankful to our teammates at The Kevin Eikenberry Group/ the Remote Leadership Institute. They are the team we learn with and from every day. Without their support and input, this book wouldn't exist, wouldn't have been finished on time, and wouldn't be as helpful as we hope you find it.

The supportive and talented team at our publishing company chose to work with us (again) and are great partners in all aspects of the publishing, editing, and marketing process. Some authors have a love-hate relationship with publishers—that is not our experience with our partners at Berrett-Koehler. To single out one individual would mean we would leave others out—we acknowledge and appreciate the entire team.

From Kevin

We stand on the shoulders of many others to get this book to you. I have been studying leadership for nearly forty years. I thank all the authors I've read, the experts I've gotten to know, and the nearly 230 experts who I learned from as the host of The Remarkable Leadership Podcast.

Personally, I must again thank our team—because they push me and challenge me to live to a higher standard every day. They deserve it and I try not to let them down.

I thank my family—my mom who taught me to be a reader, my wife Lori who loves and believes in me even when that is difficult, and my children Parker and Kelsey who continue to teach me even as they are now adults.

I am blessed beyond measure. I am grateful and aware that those blessings come from God.

From Wayne

It would be impossible to write a book like this without the candid, sometimes harsh, feedback we get from our clients. They are in the trenches every day, and I continue to learn from them while trying to make their jobs and lives easier.

It is also important to thank my peers and colleagues who are helping to chronicle the seismic changes the workplace is undergoing. These are interesting times, indeed, and we're all learning from each other.

Of course, none of this is possible without the support of The Duchess— my wife Joan—and Her Serene Highness, my daughter Nora, who will be dealing with the fallout of these changes long after I'm gone.

Index

About the Authors

Kevin Eikenberry

Kevin Eikenberry is a recognized world expert on leadership development and learning and is the Chief Potential Officer of The Kevin Eikenberry Group (KevinEikenberry.com). In the last thirty years he has worked with leaders from forty-three countries and organizations around the world.

He has been named twice by Inc.com as one of the Top 100 Leadership and Management Experts in the World and has been included in many other similar lists. He is the author, the coauthor, or a contributing author of nearly twenty books, including *Remarkable eadership, From Bud to Boss—Secrets to a Successful Transition to Remarkable Leadership* (with Guy Harris), and *The Long-Distance Leader: Rules for Remarkable Remote Leadership* (with Wayne Turmel). His blog (Blog.KevinEikenberry .com) is consistently ranked among the world's best, most read, and most shared on leadership. Contact Kevin at Kevin@KevinEikenberry.com.

Wayne Turmel

Wayne Turmel has had many careers, stand-up comic, car salesman, and cofounder of the Remote Leadership Institute among them. Throughout his working life he's been obsessed with how people communicate while working.

He's the author or coauthor of over a dozen books, including *The Long-Distance Leader: Rules for Remarkable Remote Leadership*. He is also a sought-after speaker and has worked with hundreds of clients in over seven countries.

He lives and works in Las Vegas. Marshall Goldsmith has called him "one of the unique voices in leadership."

Contact Wayne at Wayne@RemoteLeadershipInstitute.com.

About Our Services

Helping Remote Leaders and Their Teams Succeed

We're confident you found this book helpful, but we also know that it was just the tip of the iceberg. There's more to learn, and the Remote Leadership Institute is here to help. Our website gives you . . .

More tools. Our regularly updated blog shares lessons from clients and our latest thinking on the continually evolving picture of the remote working world. While there are resources you can purchase, most are completely free and ready for you to read, watch, and apply.

More learning opportunities. We offer a variety of learning opportunities for both leaders and anyone working remotely, from the unique design of "12 Weeks to Becoming a Great Remote Teammate" to the complete "Remote Leadership Certificate Series" to live, virtually delivered learning events to on-demand offerings and e-learning tools to place on your organization's LMS.

More help. If you want to talk about the broader organizational needs related to remote leadership and remote work, please reach out to us.

You can find all this and more at RemoteLeadershipInstitute.com/LDT and use promo code BOOK to receive a 25 percent discount on any of our learning products.

For all the tools available to you as a reader of this book, go to LongDistanceLeaderBook.com/resources.

More Than Leading at a Distance

This book has helped you think about the challenges and opportunities of working at a distance, but you likely have other challenges, needs, and questions too. Since 1993, The Kevin Eikenberry Group has existed to help leaders and their teams become more effective, confident, and successful. Here are some of our services.

Helping senior leaders. Need an outside perspective to reach your business goals and objectives? We help senior leaders succeed through executive coaching and consultation on building a leadership pipeline, leading culture change and change initiatives.

Helping new and frontline leaders. Do you need support for your new or first-line leaders? Through our Bud to Boss resources, we offer nearly every organizational and individual option to help your new and frontline leaders succeed. We know their challenges, opportunities, and pain, and we help hundreds of these leaders grow each year.

Helping all leaders. Are you looking to build your skills and confidence as a leader, whether you are new or have been doing this for a long time? We help all leaders with a wide variety of learning opportunities and coaching options.

Inspiring and informing teams and individuals. Are you looking for tools and options to engage and grow everyone in your organization? We offer free tools, videos, podcasts, and much more to help all employees engage and grow as a part of your organization.

Learn more at KevinEikenberry.com.

Also by Kevin Eikenberry and Wayne Turmel

The Long-Distance Leader
Rules for Remarkable Remote Leadership

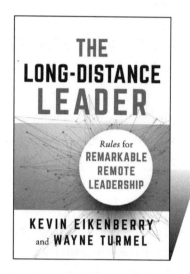

As more organizations adopt a remote workforce, the challenges of leading at a distance become more urgent than ever. The cofounders of the Remote Leadership Institute, Kevin Eikenberry and Wayne Turmel, show leaders how to guide their teams by recalling the foundational principles of leadership. The authors' "Three-O" Model refocuses leaders to think about outcomes, others, and ourselves—elements of leadership that remain unchanged, whether employees are down the hall or halfway around the world. By pairing it with the Remote Leadership Model, which emphasizes using technology as a tool and not a distraction, leaders are now able to navigate the terrain of managing teams wherever they are. Filled with exercises that ensure projects stay on track, keep productivity and morale high, and build lasting relationships, this book is the go-to guide for leading, no matter where people work.

Paperback, ISBN 978-1-5230-9461-5
PDF ebook, ISBN 978-1-5230-9462-2
ePub ebook, ISBN 978-1-5230-9463-9
Digital audio, ISBN 978-1-5230-9460-8

Berrett–Koehler Publishers, Inc.
www.bkconnection.com

800.929.2929

☸ Berrett–Koehler
BK̄ Publishers

Berrett-Koehler is an independent publisher dedicated to an ambitious mission: *Connecting people and ideas to create a world that works for all.*

Our publications span many formats, including print, digital, audio, and video. We also offer online resources, training, and gatherings. And we will continue expanding our products and services to advance our mission.

We believe that the solutions to the world's problems will come from all of us, working at all levels: in our society, in our organizations, and in our own lives. Our publications and resources offer pathways to creating a more just, equitable, and sustainable society. They help people make their organizations more humane, democratic, diverse, and effective (and we don't think there's any contradiction there). And they guide people in creating positive change in their own lives and aligning their personal practices with their aspirations for a better world.

And we strive to practice what we preach through what we call "The BK Way." At the core of this approach is *stewardship,* a deep sense of responsibility to administer the company for the benefit of all of our stakeholder groups, including authors, customers, employees, investors, service providers, sales partners, and the communities and environment around us. Everything we do is built around stewardship and our other core values of *quality, partnership, inclusion,* and *sustainability.*

This is why Berrett-Koehler is the first book publishing company to be both a B Corporation (a rigorous certification) and a benefit corporation (a for-profit legal status), which together require us to adhere to the highest standards for corporate, social, and environmental performance. And it is why we have instituted many pioneering practices (which you can learn about at www.bkconnection.com), including the Berrett-Koehler Constitution, the Bill of Rights and Responsibilities for BK Authors, and our unique Author Days.

We are grateful to our readers, authors, and other friends who are supporting our mission. We ask you to share with us examples of how BK publications and resources are making a difference in your lives, organizations, and communities at www.bkconnection.com/impact.

Dear reader,

Thank you for picking up this book and welcome to the worldwide BK community! You're joining a special group of people who have come together to create positive change in their lives, organizations, and communities.

What's BK all about?

Our mission is to connect people and ideas to create a world that works for all.

Why? Our communities, organizations, and lives get bogged down by old paradigms of self-interest, exclusion, hierarchy, and privilege. But we believe that can change. That's why we seek the leading experts on these challenges—and share their actionable ideas with you.

A welcome gift

To help you get started, we'd like to offer you a **free copy** of one of our bestselling ebooks:

www.bkconnection.com/welcome

When you claim your **free ebook**, you'll also be subscribed to our blog.

Our freshest insights

Access the best new tools and ideas for leaders at all levels on our blog at ideas.bkconnection.com.

Sincerely,

Your friends at Berrett-Koehler

Certified

Corporation